This book dramatises what the author calls:

'the daft, mundane, serious situations and predicaments of people'

It is about:

- acting, play-acting, being ourselves, being somebody else
- life and how we interact with others with whom we share it in incidental and informal ways
- what we can learn and teach about such moments
- the co-operative nature of performance
- people whose characters we get a glimpse of by watching them gesture, move and converse
- people in situations and predicaments upon whom we can impose character, or fine-tune what we 'see' as their character, by a simple change of tone, gesture, pause
- offering enlightenment, engagement and dramatic effect
- teaching it, learning about it, producing it, taking part in it
- what we can learn along the way.

At its heart are sixty short drama scripts by Edward Denniston.

For the Longford Gang – keeping shop.

INTERACTING

60 short drama scripts for
developing skills in drama, performance
and getting on with people

Edward Denniston

Russell House Publishing

First published in 2007 by:
Russell House Publishing Ltd.
4 St. George's House
Uplyme Road
Lyme Regis
Dorset DT7 3LS

Tel: 01297-443948
Fax: 01297-442722
e-mail: help@russellhouse.co.uk
www.russellhouse.co.uk

British Library Cataloguing-in-publication Data:

A catalogue record for this book is available from the British Library.

ISBN: 978-1-905541-12-6

Typeset by TW Typesetting, Plymouth, Devon
Printed and bound by Hobbs, Totton

About Russell House Publishing

Russell House Publishing aims to publish innovative and valuable materials to help managers, practitioners, trainers, educators and students.

Our full catalogue covers: social policy, working with young people, helping children and families, care of older people, social care, combating social exclusion, revitalising communities and working with offenders.

Full details can be found at www.russellhouse.co.uk and we are pleased to send out information to you by post. Our contact details are on this page.

We are always keen to receive feedback on publications and new ideas for future projects.

Contents

About the Author   vi

Index of Scripts   vii

This Book and its Possible Applications   ix
  By *Geoffrey Mann*

A Short Introduction to Using the Scripts   xiii

Help! Getting the Most Out of a Script   xv

Creative and Educational Ways of Working With Scripts   1

Ten Ways of Looking at a Script   3

Practical Notes   16

The Scripts   23

Late Night Coffee Shop: An Improvisation Exercise   155

About the Author

Edward Denniston is teacher of English, Drama and Media Studies in Newtown School, Waterford, Ireland. He has written a book of poems, *The Point Of Singing* (Abbey Press, 1999) and is member of Poetry Ireland's *Writers-in-Schools* scheme. Also, he is part of the Department of Education's *Second Level Support Service* (SLSS) for teachers of English in Ireland. He attended Trinity College Dublin and has lived and worked in Waterford since 1980.

Index of Scripts

1. Amnesia
2. Parent and Teenage Child
3. Acolyte
4. Corpse
5. Date
6. Departure
7. Divided Space
8. Filling Time
9. The Fitting Cubicle
10. Fruit in a Suitcase
11. Ghost Presence
12. Hi and Bye
13. In Love
14. Pigs and Insurance
15. Promise
16. Tell Me
17. Visit from Shakespeare
18. When to Move
19. You do Love Me
20. Dead Dog
21. Strange Meeting
22. Ways of Dying
23. Where Are You Going?
24. The Sandwich
25a. Lost in Translation
25b. Lost in Translation – French
25c. Lost in Translation – Spanish
26. Afraid of the Dark
27. Murder in the Park
28. After Friel
29. Serious Problem
30. Awkward Situation
31. Interrogation
32. Preoccupation – an Improvisation

33. What do You Want to do?
34. Yes and No
35. Gift Shop
36. Soup
37. A and B and Metaphor
38. Mirror
39. Monologue and Listener
40. Returned Visitor
41. Spoofer
42. Talk with Mother
43. Bearings
44. Explanations
45. Follow the Instructions
46. Potential Love Story in Four Seasons
47. Second-hand Books
48. Three Voices
49. A Complaint
50. Meeting of Movement
51. After Beckett
52. Elderly Couple and Ghost
53. Spacecraft
54. Worried Parent
55. Angry not Angry
56. Charity
57. I'll Phone You on Monday
58. Mystery
59. Young Child and Parent – Version 1
60. Young Child and Parent – Version 2

Note

Some of the scripts, particularly those that involve 'Dad' or 'Mum', have that gender continued through the script for clarity. Most of the scripts, however, are not gender specific and any of the parts can be male or female and neuter pronouns are used in the script.

It may be more dramatic in some circumstances to use actual names for the characters instead of just A and B.

This Book and its Possible Applications

By Geoffrey Mann, Managing Director, Russell House Publishing

At its heart this is a creative book of scripts, accompanied by material on how to use them in both formal and informal drama teaching and production. As such, we hope that you will find it to be a valuable, enjoyable and fruitful resource, whether you are:

- a school or college drama teacher
- youth arts worker
- mentor
- facilitator
- or almost anybody involved in working with young people, especially if you are concerned with helping them to reflect on how people perceive them, how they perceive other people, and how they interact with people around them.

It is useful, in each of the above cases, at all levels of experience, and with anyone who can participate in small groups. It can be used in a variety of locations: classroom, theatre, youth club or café. It can also be used with adults.

Why these scripts were written

As the author explains, 'If you, reader, are a drama teacher, facilitator, youth worker – experienced or inexperienced – in search of original scripted material for short performance, or in search of scripted material to enhance your workshop experience, then this book of short and medium length duologues and dialogues just might be what you're looking for. These scripts were borne out of the practical needs of a fellow drama teacher/facilitator who, like you, has spent quite a number of hours browsing in the *Drama Section* of book shops in search of interesting, humorous, dramatically rich, stage-craft conscious scenes and human moments (especially duologues) that aren't only extracts from plays and that don't enslave teacher and student to the endgame of the *big performance* play.'

Very human moments

These scripts, the author continues are 'scenes, or what I like to call, *very human moments* to act out and act up. Hopefully, they are practicable and stimulating and can be done in a limited space with few or no props and with basic stage furniture'.

The scripts have been intentionally created in such a way as to avoid focusing on the usual and unusual 'issues' in young people's lives, like those of bullying, parents, smoking, drugs, getting in and out of trouble, and so on. Instead they focus on the subtleties of how people interact with each other in informal, almost casual settings. This approach, in the author's words, 'allows participants, facilitators and observers to concentrate on how gesture, inflection, movement, visual messages and the unspoken, all meld together to create the fabric of human engagement (with those around us)'.

Interacting

Although it was not the author's original aim, this book thereby offers a potentially valuable contribution to responding to 'the challenge . . . to replenish society's depleted stock of skills in engaging and recognising the legitimate interests of others, of learning to challenge behaviour within a shared understanding; to hone our readiness to show consideration to others, whether we know them or not' (Kevin Harris, *Respect in the Neighbourhood*, Russell House Publishing, 2006).

In his book, Harris set up this challenge by reflecting that if 'respect' and 'neighbourliness' matter, and if there is concern that they have somehow been eroded, in our times, then 'we need to develop new skills that allow us to build respect and exercise informal control without reinstating hierarchy in the public sphere. It's not that we don't do this: it's just that we tend to avoid doing it with those with whom we have little in common. It's as if – conditioned to the taciturnity of the supermarket checkout rather than the inevitable greetings of the corner shop – we have abandoned the practice of conducting trivial interactions, because they don't matter to us. But they do matter, and we need somehow to rediscover the vernacular of mundane encounters.'

Perhaps then, these scripts can be valuable resource material in the hands of skilful facilitators in fields such as youth work, youth justice, community work, social work and social care work and in areas of formal education beyond the drama classroom.

Working with young people

Of course, there is a significant difference between drama teaching and youth drama on the one hand, and art therapy on the other. And the author of these scripts has been consistently at pains to stress that he is someone who created sixty short scripts to help in his drama teaching, and that he is not a drama therapist.

But in the same way that a youth worker, or residential worker, without in any way being a counsellor or psychologist, can help two young people to discuss why they just had an argument (how it started, what happened next, how it finished, where that leaves them, who else was affected, what they are going to do about it) so too can involving young people in a dramatised interaction help everyone concerned see into the complexities of people's interactions.

When I first, somewhat naively, suggested this to him, the author commented that 'the neighbours idea is what incidentally – and very much incidentally – happens at times when I'm dealing with these scripts with a group, say, over a ten week period. What I find is that an incidental, haphazard 'respect' emerges simply because people are being trained to focus on something outside themselves, again and again – on the text and the tasks in the text. Adults though (the ones I've dealt with!) tend to begin with a kind of exaggerated respect and deference. Adolescents, who are familiar with each other, start with a kind of bantering disrespect, which has to be renegotiated into a more formal neighbourliness or respect. Of course I always begin my drama session with the cooperative, giving, looking-out-for idea; I just don't call it respect. Whether the scripts or my style are responsible for this I can't be sure. Perhaps it's a bit of each . . . However, there's no doubt that the emphasis you suggest could be placed upon the book and the scripts could be used as an instrument to inculcate 'good' neighbourliness; and/or 'good' neighbourliness could be the incidental outcome of dealing with them over a period of time. Thinking about this now, I feel that the facilitator's attitude, feelings and ideas on drama would be central to such outcomes.'

Drama is powerful

Drama is a powerful medium. I believe that it can help to make a difference in these and perhaps other ways.

A lot can come out of a series of mundane, every-day and perfectly ordinary events, events as experienced by each and every one of us as we negotiate our lives in the context of other people.

So, although this book is not about 'serious' issues such as grief, bereavement, suicidal feelings, sexuality, being in trouble ... drama is powerful stuff, and it can provoke unexpected reactions in those who take part. As a first source of guidance to being ready for this, and to what any of us can do in specific contexts – often most importantly by making referrals and recommendations to other professionals – I recommend *Responding to Adolescents: helping relationship skills for youth workers, mentors and other advisers* (Angela Taylor, RHP 2003)

But at its heart this is a creative book of scripts, accompanied by material on how to use them in both formal and informal drama teaching and production. As such, we hope that you will find it to be a valuable, enjoyable and fruitful resource.

Geoffrey Mann,
Managing Director,
Russell House Publishing

A Short Introduction to Using the Scripts

The sixty or so scripts, the 'Ten Ways of Looking at a Script' section and the appendix are intended as a resource for illustration, discussion, learning and entertainment, and not just a collection of scripts to be read, learned and performed under time constraints, although there's no doubt that the potential for that is also there as they were written in the hope of offering entertainment, engagement and dramatic effect.

For the most part, these scripts were written:

1. For small to medium sized groups, by a drama teacher who was fully conscious of the ever-present constraints and pressures of being a teacher and facilitator – time, gender balance, ability, knowledge, entertainment etc.
2. To supplement the use of drama games and exercises with the more substantial elements of theatre: characterisation, character interaction, story, action, gesture, script writing and a sense of audience.
3. To develop a participant's understanding and awareness of the practical dynamics of acting, directing and stage work.
4. To both entertain and challenge willing participants in their effort to *play-act*.
5. To be a stimulus or catalyst for ideas and creativity from the teachers and learners point of view (see below, **Help . . .**)

Primary aim

The primary aim in creating these scripts, and behind the suggestions for use contained in the book, is to take the focus off the big play and performance and re-direct it toward the behavioural – toward the minutia of human gesture and interaction.

What are the scripts about?

These scripts are about daft, mundane, serious situations and predicaments of people (A, B and sometimes C, mostly of indeterminate gender) whose characters we get a glimpse of by watching them gesture, move and converse. Or, alternately, they are about people in situations and predicaments upon whom we can impose character, or fine-tune what we 'see' as their character, by a simple change of tone, gesture, pause etc. Many of the scripts are a glimpse at a bigger, to-be-imagined story, rather than a whole, complete story with a beginning, middle and end. This allows the facilitator and student to imagine – and perhaps write – an additional scene, one that might precede or follow the one being worked on. (See *Script Writing*, in Appendix).

While there's no doubt that these scripts are more fuelled and informed by drama, theatre, character and stage craft, than by issues and themes, it would be inaccurate to give the browsing drama teacher the impression that there is no potential for serious issues to emerge from them. *Parent and Teenage Child, Ghost Presence* and *Interrogation* are examples of this.

Here's what some of the scripts are about – this is an arbitrary selection:

Potential Love Story in Four Seasons
An elderly man and woman say roughly the same thing to each other on the street in which they live, over the time period of the four seasons. There's enough evidence in what they say and in the stage directions to suggest that one might have fallen for the other. (Page 123)

A and B and Metaphor
Here one character talks to another about a football match using some common idioms that only serves to confuse the issue. (Page 100)

Parent and Teenage Child
A parent confronts a teenager about their part in a stolen car accident in which a child was knocked off her bike. (Page 26)

When to Move
During a conversation a boy has to decide when it's best to move across a room to get closer to a girl who he likes but hardly knows. Of course this scene could be done with a same sex pair of participants. (Page 64)

I'll Phone You on Monday
A customer in a shop persists with a complaint to two shop assistants with slightly different approaches to the problem. The title is a line repeated quite often in the scene. (Page 147)

Help! Getting the Most Out of a Script

For a teacher of any discipline, new hand or old-stager, being shown *ways into* a resource can be as valuable as the resource itself. With this in mind, the *'Ten Ways of Looking at a Script'* section and the appendix and notes section have many suggestions as to the various ways in which any one script might be fully and exhaustively utilised in a session. Depending on the amount of hours you've done as a drama facilitator some of my suggestions and ideas may be familiar and obvious, although some may be new to you. Either way, as mentioned above, one of the key techniques in utilising these scripts is to take the emphasis off completion and perfection of the whole with a mind only to performance, and to sharpen the focus on word, gesture and movement in the acting space, in order to illustrate this is how story and narrative are suggested or forwarded in the theatre. Put simply, getting there, the process, should be given more emphasis than performance as an end in itself. This is not to say that completion, perfection and performance should be discouraged but only to suggest that focusing on the perfection of a small part of, or one aspect of a script maybe as satisfying as 'doing' the script as one might consider 'doing' a play. For example, to practice and perform a number of different versions of an opening exchange of lines, with accompanying gesture and movement in the stage space, might be as interesting and as fruitful as 'getting through' the script. Another example might be to experiment with the placing of silences or long pauses in one of the shorter scripts or indeed with having the characters move in a certain way as they interpret their lines.

How might participants benefit from working on these scripts in the ways suggested?

As drama teachers/facilitators we bring different emphases and theories to any one piece of dramatic material or exercise. For this teacher of adults and students, utilising these scripts (see *'Ten Ways of Looking at a Script'* section and Appendix) over the last twelve years has reinforced key aspects of the dynamics of theatre.

1. An awareness of how action and interaction on stage is about skilled cooperation between actors–even when two characters are arguing.
2. How a story is told and forwarded and audiences are influenced in the theatre by having characters talk to each other and behave in certain ways towards each other.
3. How gesture and movement can tell an audience as much as speech.
4. That to watch, listen, suggest and direct is as interesting as being on stage.
5. That physical limitation of a stage can be a stimulus to dramatic and theatrical creativity.
6. That the dynamics of dramatic experience are more complex than first thought – actor to character, actor to audience, actor to actor etc.
7. That scripts with no sound effects, no lighting (but with the potential for these) forcefully, by their absence, emphasise the powerful role they have in theatre and film.
8. That sometimes, we need to separate successful acting from the idea of star role.
9. That learning of technical terms and concepts arise from practical necessity.
10. That often, being on stage, particularly the small stage, doing less – gesture, action, talk – is often a more forceful way of revealing character.

What's for you?

Depending on your needs, you might find yourself going straight to the scripts to assess their potential as material to supplement and augment an established way of working. Alternately, a glance at the *Ten Ways of Looking at a Script* section might point you in the direction of some fresh ways of working with your class or drama group. Also, in the final section of the book, *Appendix and Notes*, there is some general advice for facilitators and teachers.

Edward Denniston

Creative and Educational Ways of Working with Scripts

The Dramatic Space

Once the space in which your drama class or workshop is to take place (see below) has been finalised, you, the teacher or facilitator, will be the first person to take command of the stage space as you address the group of participants who sit before you, in the auditorium space. In doing the above *you* become a kind of play-acting host, facilitator, improviser, questioner, illustrator.

If you or your group are new to the dynamics of theatre or drama there is a very simple but important exercise to go through before working on the scripts. So, as you stand there facing your 'audience' you might want to:

- Point out and perhaps move to, the various important positions in the space- centre stage, up stage, down stage, wings, flies etc.
- Point out and explain the limits and boundaries of the stage space and the limits of the auditorium.
- Point out when these boundaries might be broken. For example, in pantomime or when a character leaves the stage to sit in the audience while staying in character, or indeed when there's a character in the audience who interrupts or engages with what's happening on stage.

The marking out of a model theatre is a very practical way of reinforcing the magic communication line between stage space and audience. It also reinforces the notion that in live theatre an audience exerts a presence which is a catalyst for what goes on in the stage space.

(Of course all of the above can be ignored if the group with which you're working have a firm grasp of theatre dynamics and space.)

TIP. In a large, bare room, masking tape can be used to mark out the stage and auditorium space, wings, aisle etc. And even if there are no chairs, the sense of auditorium can be created by having participants sit on the floor in rows with a space in the centre to act as an aisle.

TIP. The successful setting up of the stage and auditorium space can be an exercise in itself. If participants are spread out around the room working in subgroups and you wish to reassemble the theatre space, use the command *auditorium* to have the group come together to lay out the chairs, quickly and quietly, auditorium style, in front of the marked-off stage. If this habit is instilled into your group it becomes part of the ritual business of each session.

TIP. There are a number of exercises relevant to stage and auditorium space in the appendix.

First encounter with a script

When you have established these theatre/drama lines of communication (see appendix) and wish to work on a script, you might consider some basic steps to get you started. However, the steps below in no way represent the full potential for rich engagement and learning how to deal with any one script. The remainder of this section deals with more specific ideas for utilising the dialogue and duologue material.

Versions and variations of the following stages are suggested here to give a kind of basic methodology:

1. Read the script in silence. Then, volunteers read parts aloud. Allow time for comments, questions and observations.
2. Another reading of the script in subgroups with participants focusing on the whole script or one of the ideas or tasks suggested in the section *Dealing With the Scripts –Ideas, Questions, Tasks*.
3. Regroup in auditorium space. Subgroups play out part or all of the script for their peers in the acting space. Or they present their version of the task set (see above).
4. Feed back, discussion, suggestions after each subgroup or all subgroups present a version.

(Remember: Having each subgroup deal with a different script is an option. If this is done it means that at Stage 1 the whole group will be reading a number of scripts.)

Ten Ways of Looking at a Script

These are the ideas and tasks to which a subgroup might apply itself during Stage 2 (see above). The suggestions under each heading are in no way complete.

Hopefully though, they will help to focus on the brief. In many scripts much will be left up to the players and director to decide upon; in others, the stage directions are very specific. Of course, in order to focus on one aspect of a script it is vital that some time be given to discussing the scene in its entirety.

TIP. Always bear in mind and always remind your participants and students to do the same: **less might mean more** when being a character on stage. Or, to put it another way, too much action and gesture on a stage merely confuses an audience and no one action or gesture is seen as important to the scene.

TIP. During the replay stage, when the subgroups have discussed and rehearsed don't forget, as teacher or facilitator, you can take command of the stage and ask the 'audience' for comments and suggestions about the characters they saw (not the actors) and what they did and didn't do.

1. Beginnings

Discuss, offer suggestions and rehearse versions of a script's opening. What's meant by *beginning* is: the opening scene-setting paragraph, if there is one, and (depending on length) about the first two, four or six speeches of a script including stage directions. Here are a number of questions to help participants focus on a beginning:

- Who is on stage? Who should be on stage when the scene begins?
- Who enters first?
- What is the character feeling as they enter the situation?
- Will they be hiding a feeling from another character?
- How does a character enter? How will they walk? Will they walk?
- What facial expression will they have?
- From where does a character enter?
- What gesture from a character do you want an audience to notice?
- What distance do you want between characters?
- Will there be silences, pauses?
- How might an audience judge a character based on this opening?

Some suggestions: *In Love; Murder in the Park; You do Love me; Date; A Complaint; Yes and No; Where Are You Going?; Departure.*

Tasks

- Have each subgroup work on two contrasting versions of a beginning. The contrast might focus on tone of voice, gesture, volume, stage direction, accent, one less serious than the other, etc.
- Or simply have each subgroup perform its version of the beginning of a script.

2. Endings

Discuss, offer suggestions and rehearse versions of a script's ending.

What I mean by *ending* is: (depending on length) the last two, four or six speeches of a script, including stage directions. The script itself may answer some of the following questions. Again, the questions are to help focus on the task in hand:

- Will the scene end with an empty stage?
- If not, who is to be left on stage?
- What does each character feel at the end?
- Where does a character exit?
- How, physically, do they exit?
- Why are they exiting at this point?
- Does the character remaining watch them exit?
- Does the character exiting look back?
- Could a final line be said off stage, the character having exited?
- What impression do we want a character to leave with an audience?
- How is a last line to be said?
- What final gesture or facial expression should a character make?

Some suggestions: *Awkward Situation; Mystery; Murder in the Park; When to Move; Departure; Pigs and Insurance; Worried Parent.*

Tasks

- Each subgroup performs for the rest of the group two contrasting versions of an ending, with guidance (see *tasks* above). Each subgroup simply performs its version of an ending.

- Alternately, each subgroup might re-write the final four speeches of the script with stage direction for rehearsal and performance in front of the whole group. (see *Appendix and Notes* for script writing suggestions).

3. Silence/Pause

This work is probably more manageable with one of the shorter scripts. Read and discuss the script. Then re-read, paying particular attention to where the silences and pauses are written in by the scriptwriter. The following questions might help when examining the silences and pauses in a script:

- Why has the silence come about? Try to explain, given the context and what's said.
- Which character is actually being silent or hesitating? Be precise.
- What does each character think or feel in the silence or pause? Be precise.
- What gestures or actions should happen in the silence or pause?
- Does a character look at anything during the silence?
- Where does a character fix their gaze during the pause?

Some suggestions: *A Complaint; A and B and Metaphor; Monologue and Listener; What do You Want to do?; Mystery.*

Tasks

- Have one subgroup play or read the scene with no silences or pauses and another to do so with them included.
- Introduce two or three silences or long pauses into a script and give two reasons as to why each occurs at this particular point in the scene.
- Ask the characters to freeze in a silence or pause. Then ask each in turn to say what they're now feeling or thinking as characters.

4. Turning Points

Again, using the stages set out in *First Encounter*, get the group to read a script, (see suggestions below) asking volunteers to read the parts. Then, break up into subgroups to have the script re-read and discussed with a view to finding turning points in it. A turning point might be defined as follows: a clearly identifiable moment in the script, or suggested by the script, that an audience might notice in performance – a moment of change. This can be a change of feeling, mood, behaviour, language, attitude, pace, fact etc. Some turning points are more obvious than others. If you think you've found a turning point the following questions might be asked:

- What's the nature of the turning point? Has it to do with language, mood, how a character feels, and action or gesture, new information?
- Which character is responsible for the turning point?
- Does the change affect where a character moves to in the stage space?
- Is there a specific gesture, action, word or tone that might reveal this turning point to an audience?
- Does the turning point change the relationship between the people on stage? For example, does the dominant character become in any way less dominant?

Some suggestions: *Returned Visitor; When to Move; Angry Not Angry; Bearings; Spoofer.*

Tasks

- Pinpoint exactly in the script where the turning point occurs. Having discussed what kind of turning point it is, rehearse the moment that leads up to it and the moment immediately after it (**important**: don't perform whole script).
- Have one member of the subgroup inform the audience about the kind of turning point they've identified. Perform a version of it or perform two contrasting versions of it to the gathered group.

5. The Listener
Some scripts in the book lend themselves to 'listener' work more than others. However, taking a closer look at the listener is interesting. The listener might be seen as some or all of the following: the character who listens during a longish speech; the character who obviously speaks the least in the scene or the one who doesn't speak at all; the listener can also be seen as the one who hasn't initiated the conversation; they listen and have to respond. Have a silent reading of the script by everyone followed by a volunteer reading, aloud.

Break into subgroups and ask them to do further readings but this time ask them to think about and focus on the listener, what is meant by a listener and what they do and might do as they are being spoken to. To help focus on the listener, the following questions might be asked:

- Who is the listener and who is the talker?
- Do the listener's feelings change as the script progresses?
- Is there anywhere in the script where it seems that the listener could say something but they decide not to?
- Is the listener the dominant one in the conversation?
- What does the talker want the listener to feel?
- What does the listener want the talker to feel?
- Is the listener actually interested in what is being said?
- Why is the listener listening? Be precise.

(In the case of some scripts the answers to the above might not be so obvious or clear cut.)

Some suggestions: *Preoccupation; Parent and Teenage Child; A Story in Four Seasons; Gift Shop; Dead Dog; Ghost Presence; Monologue and Listener.*

Tasks

- Get the subgroups to agree some very definite and clearly directed gestures, movements and expressions for the listener; act them out (the fewer the better).
- Also, get the subgroups to agree on what the listener's dominant feeling might be as they listen.
- Rehearse using all or part of a script and then perform to the group. See if the rest of the group, as an audience, can guess what this dominant feeling is?

6. Character

Similar to a story line or 'what happens' in a script, discussion about character is a more obvious and familiar way of looking at a script for participants in a drama workshop. Again, use the stages mentioned above to begin your exploration of character: gather the group in the set out auditorium; stand before them as facilitator and have a silent reading of a script and then a reading aloud, relying on volunteers to take on the parts.

You might point out to the assembled participants that you're not acting out a character's part, but you are in the role of teacher or facilitator.

Perhaps when looking at character, a number of readings should be done, getting as many people as possible to take on the parts of A, B – and sometimes – C. Once the reading aloud has been done with volunteers from the whole group break up into subgroups in order to re-read, discuss and rehearse the script, this time with full focus on the characters that emerge in the action and speech. Once again, a number of vital questions will help students to get a sense of the complexity of the character they want to see and hear in the acting space:

- From the audience's point of view, what feelings does this character seem to have?
- How familiar will these characters be with each other?
- What is the relationship between the characters?
- Does a character feel differently at the end of the encounter?
- What does one character *want* another character to feel as they talk to them?
- What feelings (if any) does a character want to keep hidden from those listening (excluding the audience)?
- As far as you can judge from the details of the script, what motivates each character in the situation?
- In performance, which character will come across more sympathetically?
- Based on a character's behaviour, language and gesture in the scene, what character traits best describe them?
- What two gestures, not in the stage directions, might best convey these traits?
- Which character is more in charge of the situation? Is this maintained? What movement, gestures, way of speaking might be used to create a clear contrast between characters?
- How do you want a character to move in the stage space? What's their demeanour, their physicality? How do they sit? How do they stand?

Some suggestions: *Elderly Couple; In Love; I'll Phone You on Monday; A Story in Four Seasons; Talk With Mother; Worried Parent; Three Voices; Returned Visitor; Fitting Cubicle.*

Tasks

- Read, discuss, rehearse and perform a full script where the sole aim is to emphasise the contrast between two characters.
- Take a short script or part of a longer one; read, discuss and perform two versions of one character, a sympathetic one and a less sympathetic one. Give the audience a chance to decide which is which.
- Perform a script or part of one with contrasting accents.
- Rehearse and perform a version of the script in which one character has a very obvious behaviour that they repeat; for example clasped hands, touching of nose, closed eyes when speaking.
- Before rehearsing a script give the characters a job, a specific age, an income, a marital status, a dwelling etc. and let this govern how the character acts and speaks.
- Get actors to freeze at the point in the script where there's the most tension: ask each to say what they are thinking and feeling at that moment.

TIP. When exploring the whole idea of character on stage, it is a good idea for a facilitator to break into a performance, when the opportunity arises, to point out any behaviour and gesturing that might be overly familiar, given that the characters on stage are meant to be a stranger to each other.

TIP. Depending on the scene, it may be advisable sometimes to limit how close actors come towards each other. This instruction counteracts the tendency of inexperienced actors to drift towards each other as they act out their lines.

TIP. Ask the subgroups to agree on first and second names for A, B and C.

7. Going elsewhere in the story

This is a natural follow on from the work on character. In this exercise, following a group reading aloud, ask the subgroups to re-read the script and make suggestions as to the story behind the scene. The questions that might help focus on this are:

- If what is going on is only suggested by the script, can the subgroup come to some agreement as to what is precisely going on?

- What are the ages of the characters?
- What is their situation – work, home, education?
- What's the story outside this scene?
- What kind of family does each come from?

Some suggestions: *Gift Shop* (see Appendix and Notes); *After Friel; Returned Visitor; Soup; Visit From Shakespeare.*

Tasks

- Have subgroups invent **one** short scene that takes place before **or** after the scene depicted in the script. It must be one scene. Come to an agreement and be specific about the time gap between the improvised scene and the script scene.
- Discuss, rehearse and perform for the main group the additional short improvised scene. Try to stay loyal to the character types.
- Write a script of the scene imagined and improvised. (See *Appendix and Notes* for some ideas on script writing)

TIP. Remind members of the group that improvisation is ultimately about cooperation even though characters may be opposed to each other.

TIP. When working with inexperienced improvisers it's always best to set limits. For example: no more than two characters in the scene; no more than three to four speeches for each character; keep the speeches fairly short; one character must enter first; one must leave first; there must be a silence or long pause.

TIP. Instead of improvising another scene that comes before or after the script being dealt with, the participants could write the scene, using the lay out and style of the scripts as a creative model.

8. The issue:

Not all scripts have an obvious issue fuelling the exchanges between the characters and where this is the case, an issue or subject can be imposed or read into the script. The issue then can be a point of discussion and the reading, rehearsal and performance can be governed by the outcome. Asking a number of questions about the issue might help:

- What exactly is the issue? Be precise.
- Is it more of an issue for one character than another?

- What kind of issue is it – moral, religious, social, creative, personal etc.?
- What are the opposing stands on the issue? Be precise.
- Is any one character hiding, from another character, their real view and attitude towards the issue?
- Is there a resolution?
- Does one want a resolution more than the other?
- Where, when the script is performed, will the issue be most strongly felt by an audience? Identify the moment.
- If there's no issue, what motivates the conversation?

Some suggestions: *Dead Dog; Young Child and Parent, version 1 and 2; Acolyte; Yes and No; Tell Me; Fruit in a Suitcase; Returned Visitor; Interrogation.*

9. Directing

One of the interesting outcomes from subgroups who work on the scripts is that those more interested in directing than acting get a say as to what actually happens in the acting space. And it is valuable, at the level of a subgroup, to read a script from a director's point of view. A director will have a more definite interpretation of the script and will understand the effect they want to communicate to the audience. They will be interested in an overview. A director of a script might ask the following questions, before rehearsal:

- What one, two or three (no more) essential qualities of the script must come across to an audience – humour, madness, character difference, specific emotion, kinds of movement, mood etc.?
- Is there anything specific that a character's hand should be doing as they speak, generally, or during a particular speech?
- What tones of voice can be heard in the lines?
- How will I use the space? Where will the characters stand or sit?
- What couple of natural gestures might help reveal the characters?
- When will eye contact be really important?
- What two adjectives describe each character?
- What can be done to ensure that the gesture, action and speech all look and sound natural and undirected?
- Given what's said and done in the script what are each character's feelings?

- What feelings, if any, are the characters trying to hide?
- How will an audience sense/understand this 'hiding'?

Some suggestions: *Three Voices* (for facial expression especially), *Where are You Going?; Yes and No* (potential for movement in the stage space); *Awkward Situation; Lost in Translation; Pigs and Insurance.*

Tasks

- Give one participant the responsibility of being the director in a subgroup. Have their version performed.
- Have two directors do a version each, with the same actors.
- Following a group reading, during which the focus has been on directing, reassemble the whole group for a directing session; have actors play the opening or closing moments of a script; take suggestions from the auditorium and have the section repeated taking on some of the suggestions. Facilitate a discussion about the effects of the changes.
- In preparing part or all of a script for a performance ask each subgroup to come to an agreement on two or three subtle, clearly defined but relevant directions which the actors (who may be the directors also) use in performance. After each subgroup's perform-ance, ask members of the audience if they noticed any specific or striking stage direction that had been introduced for one of the characters.
- Write a script of three speeches for two characters in which there are five very specific stage directions for each character.

TIP. Spend some time on getting across the message that actors agree to be governed by the member of the group who is playing the role of director.

TIP. In the exercise where directing suggestions are taken from the audience it's a good idea if the suggestion is accompanied by one or two reasons based on the script or interpretation of character.

TIP. For those new to the idea of seeing acting and performance from the directing point of view, choose a very short script or a short extract from a long script.

10. Complete performance
With any group of enthusiastic participants or students the desire to learn and perfect one favourite script will manifest itself. The

subgrouping might be on the basis of interest, and those who are most keen on directing might be given the role of director, overseen, as they work, by the facilitator. The budding director and the actors might consider a few questions:

- What are the one or two essential qualities in the script that should come out in performance?
- What is the script about or what happens in the script that an audience should be clear on?
- Where is the turning point, or points, in the script?
- What emotion fuels each character?
- What sound effects might go with the performance?
- What few props would help with the performance?

Tasks

- Ask the whole group to agree about four to five criteria on which to judge each performance of a script. Scale the criteria from one to five. Ask the audience to mark their score sheet after they watch each performance.
- Same as above only each subgroup does the same script.

Ten Ways of Looking at a script

20: Dead Dog

A and B (with newspaper) are strangers sitting at the same table in a coffee shop. A can be an elderly woman or man. B is a middle-aged person of either gender. For a while both are in their own separate worlds but the elderly A is a little agitated and upset. B gradually becomes aware of this before A speaks.

A. *(Stares at B for a while before speaking)* Excuse me?

B. Yes.

A. I wonder would you be able to help me?

B. *(Cautiously)* Yes?

A. My dog died.

B. Oh dear, I'm sorry to hear that. *(Attempts to return to coffee and newspaper)*

Much time can be spent on how one acts a 'little agitated' and how one might become 'gradually aware', in a natural way. Versions of the unworded parts of the scripts can be acted out.

This line is a surprise to B and to the audience. It asks for a reaction from both. Always be on the look out for these in a script. Distinguish between the character's appropriate response and its effect on the audience.

There are other ways to open this scene. Perhaps A enters after B? Focus on how this opening is to be done before moving on. Pay attention to the detail – 'agitated', 'separate worlds'.

Adhere to stage directions unless they simply don't work. Then, blame the writer.

Here, in the script we *hear* a pause. In the pause, there is a gesture. Listen out for these in all scripts.

This moment in the scene is a kind of turning point. Look out for these in other scripts, major and minor. There are many kinds of turning points.

Look out for other speeches like this, in other scripts. A speech in which one character wants another to feel in a particular way; and this feeling they hope will be of benefit.

A scene can end with a gesture or grand action. If a character/s remains on stage use the 5 second freeze as a way of 'bringing down the curtain or lights'.

(*Pause*)

A. Could you help me?

B. (*Trying to keep it vague*) Sorry?

A. Would you be able to help me? (*Looks straight at B*) I'd be very…… grateful.

B. (*Before speaking, he looks around the coffee shop to see if anyone's listening*) I'm not sure. I have to go very soon.

A. This won't take a minute. You see Rex died in the living room and I'm on the fourth floor over there (*Pointing into auditorium*) and I can't get him down. (*Brief pause*) I want to get him into the back garden where I have a lovely plot for him you see – under the old apple tree. (*A is silenced with disbelief that this is happening to him*) It wouldn't take you long at all.

Be clear about what happens in a pause. The attention is on act and gesture.

This script has no 'directed' ending. The scene is not over with the last spoken word – no scene is. At the end of a scene what do we want an audience to *see*? Here, B has to speak. A and/or B have to leave.

Practical Notes

Groups and subgroups

When using these scripts a manageable group size is between 12 and 18. The greater the number, the longer it takes to get through each performance; however, the larger number does give a sense of audience for the performers.

Learning off by heart

One of the ways of encouraging participants that lines can be learnt off by heart is to deal with sections of a script – the opening or closing four speeches for example. Then move on to a short script. My experience is that an initial success at learning off lines whets the appetite, especially when participants realise the freedom that comes from not having to carry a book or sheet around.

Questioning and discussion

When, as facilitator, you question your students about performing the scripts, it's a good idea to refer to A, B and C as character and not refer to the actor. For example, *'Would you like to see A come on first? 'Do you think this character should move away at this point' 'Does this character want to look away at this moment'* etc. This reinforces drama's sense of immediacy and it takes the focus off the actors.

What's not in the script

These scripts don't have sound effects, lighting suggestions or music and they demand minimal stage furniture. However, because of this, they may be useful for the drama teacher or facilitator who wishes to explore production values with a group.

Improvisation

Improvisation is very difficult for some participants but it is always worth doing even at a very basic level. Before asking students to do any, however, emphasise the point that success lies in cooperation between two actors, conspiring together to make an impact on an audience. Try to dispel the notion that it is about competition between actors – although at times it can be. Here are a number of exercises that might help to emphasise the idea of cooperation:

Exercise 1
Ask two willing and enthusiastic participants in a group to have a three to four minute conversation (use a stop watch) in the stage space on any given subject or issue; however, towards the end they must get across to an audience that a disagreement is *beginning to emerge*. The three to four minutes must be up before each character becomes very adamant with the other. Allow them a few minutes to prepare.

Exercise 2
Character A and character B are in the stage space. A asks B to leave. B's job is to refuse convincingly and then relent, and leave convincingly. The relent must sound and look plausible. A's job is to offer B lines that allow them to relent convincingly. This must happen within the space of one minute. It is the job of the two participants to do this in as natural and convincing a way as possible.

Exercise 3
A is drunk and is removed physically from the stage by B who is a bouncer very aware of litigation. A must act out their physical resistance in a convincing way and they must act out being overpowered in a convincing way. Again, this should have a time limit of about one minute. Give participants time to prepare.

Script writing
As part of the work dealing with these scripts, it is worthwhile having a script writing session where the students produce their own scripts. If they can word-process and produce a final draft, all the better. In my experience the method of giving parameters and prescription leads to better writing and more effective scripts:

Layout

- about 2cm margin between speaker's name and their speech
- generous line spacing (one and a half)
- double spacing between speakers

- agree on a font size (12 or 14 point)
- agree on an unfussy font type
- put stage directions in brackets and italics
- put stage directions in the present tense

Other (choose any combination)

- no more than two or three characters
- set a limit for the length of speeches
- set limit for the number of speeches (five for each character)
- the script must have a turning point
- one of the characters must be hiding their feelings
- one of the characters must have a secret
- a character must leave the stage space and return
- there must be one long silence in the dialogue
- a small prop must be used
- one character must try to convince the other
- a lie must be found out in the encounter

Stage Space Exercise 1

Step 1

Give out a list of the following stage positions to your drama group who are in the devised auditorium (see *The Dramatic Space*): **down stage centre, down stage left, down stage right, up stage centre, up stage right, up stage left, exit left, exit right, exit aud** (auditorium).

Step 2

Make up two or three pairs from the group, depending on the area size of acting space. One from each pair (the Caller) stays in the auditorium and the other (the Mover) takes up a position in the stage space. For about half a minute each the Caller must call out a stage position to their Mover who must respond immediately. If Exit is called the Mover must go off stage; or, if the space is too cramped to have an off stage left or right, they must go to the edge of the stage space and stand perfectly still until the next stage position call. The focus and aim for the Mover is to move quickly and deftly and avoid all contact with the others doing the same in the stage space, especially if they end up at the same stage position. Competition will arise as Movers will want to get to the best position first.

Step 3

There are various embellishments to this exercise. One is to have the Mover, on arrival at the position to shout 'Here' or 'Got it'. Another is to have the Caller and Mover speak with accents or in various tones.

Also, the Mover could be asked to move in a certain way.

Stage Space Exercise 2

Step 1

Ask two or three 'actors' to take up a 'hiding' position in the stage space (they are hiding from each other). They must move from the auditorium space into the stage space as if trying to avoid being seen. Obviously, while there's nowhere to hide, each must convince themselves that they are hiding from the others. Above all, they must avoid eye contact with the others in the space and the audience.

Step 2

When they've been in their hiding position for about thirty seconds each must then move – hiding, keeping low – in the stage space, trying to go everywhere in it without being 'seen'. The hider, at all costs must **act** unaware of the others in the space. A variation of this is to have two people enter the stage space from opposite wings and sneak and hide their way to the opposite wing, ignoring each other as they meet and pass. The two participants should be encouraged to use the full depth of the space and to be inventive as they make their way across. The audience can then be asked what gestures and expressions they found most convincing. To talk about gesture, movement, expression takes attention to the actual participant.

Stage Space Exercise 3

Very simply, divide the main group into two. Ask each subgroup to go away and devise a curtain call for the end of a play, using the entries, exits and stage space creatively and inventively. Following some rehearsal time, each of the subgroups presents its curtain call. The prompt for entry into the stage space is the clapping from the second subgroup who play the role of audience.

Characters Exercise

Step 1
Paper and pens and a batch of newspapers will be required for this exercise, one newspaper for each member of the group. Ask each participant to read the news stories that don't involve a celebrity, politicians or any famous person they might know. Choose a newspaper article that is of interest or intriguing.

Step 2
Then, in turn, using the details of the news report in front of them ask each member of the group to tell their story by being the person in the report (i.e. the first person mode will be used). Stress the importance of proper nouns. As well as giving details in the report they may add other plausible details. Also, they must say where they are now (location, a time) at this precise moment (for example, they might tell their story from a prison cell or from a holiday resort apartment). The incident in the newspaper can be in their past.

Step 3
Going around the group again, ask each character to say how they feel now about the incident that got them into the news and about others who were affected by the incident. Ask them to explain how the incident came about.

Step 4
Having listened to the stories the facilitator might question some of those who are not being specific enough with information, or about how they feel. This can be done during stages 2 and 3.

Step 5
Give out a small sheet of paper to each participant. Ask each one to imagine a scenario in which their character and one other (from the group of characters) might be likely to meet up. It is important here to be specific: exact location, time of day, season, reasons for being there. Write these details in the present tense.

Step 6

In pairs, prepare and then act out an improvised scene between the two characters. Or, individually, write a short script of the encounter (see script writing guidelines).

Lines of communication

From time to time it is important to remind those involved in rehearsal, performance, directing and production that there are quite a few lines of communication going on at any one time. Here are some of the important ones:

- actor to actor (on and off stage)
- character to character
- outer character to inner character (see *After Friel*)
- character to actor, actor to character
- character to audience directly (pantomime, aside, soliloquy, over-acting, up-staging)
- character to audience indirectly (the audience are eavesdroppers)
- director to actor, actor to director
- character to director
- production (sound effects, music, set, design) to audience

Suggestions for Going Elsewhere Exercise
(see *Ten Ways of Looking . . .*)

No. 1

Having had a reading of *Gift Shop,* consider the following: the scene is actually part of a murder story. The shopkeeper plans to murder their spouse in the near future. Invent motives for the intended crime. Then, imagine a scene where the shopkeeper is having tea with their spouse after the shop shuts. The rude customer who didn't purchase anything comes up in the conversation. Improvise the scene or write some dialogue for it.

No. 2

Having read through *Returned Visitor,* ask the students to 'go to' what they imagine to be the next scene in the story. Write some dialogue for this scene or improvise it. Alternately, imagine a scene that has happened in the past, in which the man in the story and the older sister finally go their separate ways. Again, improvise this scene or write dialogue for it.

Notes for the Facilitator or Teacher

As a scene is being played out always be ready to intervene. Here are a few reasons for intervention:

- To illustrate an effective action, gesture, tone, pause.
- To point out why what has happened might be implausible.
- To ask that a successful moment be replayed.
- To point out that an actor is too conscious of an audience.
- To talk to the audience about a character (not an actor).
- To have a character speak of their feelings at a particular moment.
- To ask the audience for an alternative stage direction.

It is very important to remind participants that when they are in character they must get the measure of how familiar or unfamiliar they should be with another character, given the situation and the relationship suggested by the script. For example, what's the difference in terms of distance between standing beside a stranger in the queue and standing beside a friend?

In your drama class, establish certain rituals or habits. For example, establishing the auditorium and stage space, calling freeze to allow for intervention, repeating the same few warm up exercises.

Remind participants that they are playing 'for' and necessarily 'to' an audience.

If some members of the group are new to drama and performance, ask that they participate in the subgroups but that they can remain in the audience and opt out of performance for a while.

Ask that each group elect or nominate a spokesperson that will communicate their ideas to the facilitator as they rehearse.

Constantly remind participants to use the stage space fully. Do let them walk towards each other as they say their lines.

At the end and beginning of each performance insist on a five second freeze/silence.

Ask participants to get into the habit of asking the two questions: Why does a character move like this or make this gesture at this particular moment? Why precisely do they speak these words, at this moment?

Take the opportunity to participate yourself. Perform.

The Scripts

1: **Amnesia**

A.   As I was saying, Sam, he aaaa . . . *(Somehow forgetting)*

B.   *(Waits for A to finish)* Yeah?

A.   What?

B.   Sam – you were saying about Sam.

A.   Was I?

B.   Yeah. You were going to say something about Sam.

A.   *(Confused)* What?

B.   What do you mean, what?

A.   I was thinking. Mmmmm. *(Thinks)*

B.   Just tell me what you were saying.

A.   Saying?

B.   Yes, about Sam.

A.   Sam.

B.   Yes, Sam.

A.   What I was saying was that he was . . .

B.   I got that bit. What was he? *(Long pause. A, more baffled)* You were telling me about Sam.

A.   Telling *you*?

B.   Yes. *You* were telling *me* about *him*, Sam.

A.   I don't remember.

B.   What do you mean you don't remember?
     (Silence. Both try to get a grip of the conversation so far)

A.   What was it?

B.   What was what?

A.   What was it I was saying that I forgot – I mean what were we saying about . . . *(trails off)*

B. When, when?

A. Before I got to where I can't remember. We were talking.

B. Yes, we were talking.

A. Well, what was it? *(Pause)* Just tell me. *(Pause)* Before, when we started.

B. We talked about something and then we . . .

A. Yeah, go on.

B. And we went on to mention how . . .

A. Just tell me what you said before we got to what I was saying.

B. About Sam.

A. Yes. *(Pause)* Well tell me.

B. We were saying . . . aaaa . . . let me see . . .

A. Come on, come on and I'll tell you exactly . . .

B. Stop!

A. What?

B. What was I saying before you started to tell me. What was it?

A. How the hell should I know?

B. You're impossible. *(Exit. A sits on, confused)*

2: Parent and Teenage Child

A (parent) and B (teenage child) enter from stage left amid fairly heated conversation. A enters first with B following. There are two chairs and a table in the room.

A.   Let me get this straight again. This . . . What's-his-name
. . .?

B.   Joey.

A.   *(Points to chair. B sits. A remains standing)* Sit down.
This could take a while. Joey – your friend Joey – pulls up
in his car . . . Where does he pull up in his car?

B.   Pond Street.

A.   He pulls up in his car at Pond Street –the park end of
course, where all the misjudged youth 'hang out' – was it?

B.   Yeah.

A.   So this character Joey pulls up at the park in *his* – or *a* car
– and you get in and you drive out to Mill Lake. Oh, and he
stops on the way, for – Jane? And then the three of you
head off. Is that right?

B.   Yea, that's what I said.

A.   Look, don't get tetchy with me. I'm trying to get this story
right because you and I just might have to tell it quite a
few times before the week is out. Do you understand?
(Pause) Did you tell the policewoman what you told me?

B.   Yes, I did.

A.   Did you tell her anything else? *Should* you have told her
anything else?

B.   No, I don't think so.

A.   And the second question?

B.   What do you mean?

A. *(Exasperated)* Is there anything you really should have told her that just might look as if what you first said was selective story telling?

B. No. I tried to tell her everything.

A. For example, did this girl – Jane – sit in the front or the back.

B. In the front. I sat in the back.

A. Did you tell the police that?

B. I can't remember – I think so.

A. And now it seems that this Jane is more fond of Joey than you, doesn't it?

B. She's lying. They're both lying.

A. It's two against one laddybuck, two against one. As far as Jane and Joey – your friends – are concerned, the three of you sat in the park, got an idea to steal a car and stole it from outside the panel-beaters.

B. It's just not true. I was seen at the park gate.

A. Oh yeah, and the misjudged youth will rush forward in your support, I suppose. Do you know what that means?

B. What?

A. You stealing the car.

B. I didn't have anything to do with stealing the car.

A. It means that you're just a little more implicated in knocking that young girl off her bike than you care to think. *(Pause, as if to get home the idea)* It wasn't Joey's car that hit her. It was a car stolen by you and the others – that's the way it could look. *(Sees that B is about to react to this)* Look, don't get all excited with me. That's the way it could look.

B. But I wasn't with them. *(Pause. Silence)* I wasn't. I thought it was his car, or his brother's car.

A.   Don't respond to what I'm about to say, okay? *(Pause)* Part of me is thinking – you could be using me to lie your way to an easier conscience. *(Pause)* Was the young girl awake when they put her in the ambulance?

B.   Yeah, she looked okay. *(Long pause)* She cried for a bit and then stopped.

A.   *(Thinking ahead)* She cried. Of course she bloody cried. *(Pause)* Bloody hell.

B.   We weren't going fast.

A.   You hit her. *(Loudly, with hand clap)* Bang! And she hit the road. *(Pause)* She's in hospital.

B.   Don't keep saying that – *I* didn't hit her.

A.   *(Looks at B, checking)* You may as well have as far as I'm concerned. *(B gets up to leave the room. Almost aggressive)* Sit down, will you. *(More controlled)* Don't go anywhere for the moment. *(Pause)* Do you know what you're going to do now – right now?

B.   *(Looks at A for answer)* What?

A.   Phone the hospital. Phone and ask about her. And then go there and meet her parents, or whoever's there worried bloody sick about what the horrible outcome might be.

B.   *(Pause)* Will I?

A.   Yes, you will. You'll phone them first – that's my advice to you.

B.   Will you come with me?

A.   *(Briefly considers)* No, I won't. No, you do this. *(Pause)* God almighty, I just hope you're right. Did she get up?

B.   No.

A.   Did they put one of those spine brace things on her?

B.   No. I don't think so.

A.   Get the number. Phone. And get ready to go to the hospital.

B. *(Getting up)* What if her parents . . .?

A. Just get the number, will you.

B. *(Exiting)* But . . .?

A. Look, would you hurry up. You're meant to be concerned for her, not yourself. *(Pause. Shouts after B who is off stage at this point)* I'll drive you to casualty – okay? *(Sits on)*

3: Acolyte

A and B are in an art gallery. The four sides of the acting space, including the invisible wall between the auditorium and stage, are the walls of the gallery. As this is being performed, B's admiration and respect for A should be communicated by tone, gesture and movement. The relationship between A and B could be romantic or simply one of hero worship.

A and B scan the walls separately. This takes quite a while and is done without either speaking. The picture that A has been struck by is on the 'wall' between the audience and stage space.

A.   Look at this one. It's extraordinary. *(B, who has been examining the paintings on another wall, goes to stand beside A)* Look at the way the body emerges from the blur of colour.

B.   Yea, it's good. *(Pause)* It's got no head.

A.   Yes, it's as if it's about to appear at any moment. Perhaps that's the point.

B.   I like the bright colours. Have a look at this one over here – a blue open mouth. *(B walks ahead of A with enthusiasm, while A strolls behind, taking in the whole room. This painting might be on one of the wing walls)* What do you think? *(Pause)* Isn't it good?

A.   *(In a dead pan way)* It's interesting.

B.   I think it's very good.

A.   *(Moving to another one on the auditorium wall)* This one is very different from the rest.

B.   *(Still looking at 'the open mouth', B is restless and bored)* Shall we move onto the next room?

A.   *(Doesn't answer immediately. Engrossed in the picture)* No, no, I'm going to have another look at these. You go ahead.

B.   *(Obviously not sharing A's interest or engagement)* Yeah, maybe I'll take another look. *(Pause)* It's a good exhibition, isn't it?

A.   *(Following quite a long study of a particular painting, A begins to exit, slowly and in thought)* Amazing. Just amazing. *(B follows doing their best not to appear bored)*

4: Corpse

The acting space is a room in a large house. It is night. The room is pitch black. A and B act accordingly. They have broken into a house to reclaim a piece of property that rightly belongs to them, which for some reason, they can't reclaim honestly. They enter, stage left, groping in the dark. On a table, unknown to A and B, in the centre of the room, there's a corpse, its head facing down stage, its feet upstage. A and B whisper loudly. This loud whispering is maintained throughout the episode but A finds it difficult and at times lapses into normal volume.

   Obviously, A and B can be either male or female.

A.   What room is this?

B.   Drawing room – I think.

A.   How do you know?

B.   Second door, right of hall door.

A.   Okay, let's get this over with and get out of here. This is crazy.

B.   Where are you?

     (A and B follow each other's voice)

A.   Here.

B.   Where?

A.   Over here. *(They touch)* Shit!

B.   Shhhh. You go round the other way. Follow the walls.

A.   Christ, this is spooky.

B.   Go on. Go that way. *(Pointing)*

A.   Whadaya mean, 'that way'. I can't see a bloody thing.

B.   Clockwise, clockwise. And keep your voice down.

A.   Let's stay together.

B.   No. Go on.

A. Right. Clockwise. *(They head off in opposite directions around the room, tentatively, groping, feeling their way in the dark)* See you back here.

B. Very funny. *(B moves around the space, firstly moving upstage left and then across the back of the space, obviously unaware of C)*

A. *(Moves downstage left and then across the front of the space)* Anything?

B. What?

A. Anything?

B. No.

A. How do you know it's here?

B. It's here. Just look.

A. Feel, you mean.

B. We can't miss it.

A. Pitch dark and we can't miss it!

B. Keep your voice down, will you. *(B moves across the back of the space towards stage right. They then move down stage right and across the front of the space, passing A unawares. They feel their way upstage left and turn in towards the centre of the room)* It must be here somewhere. It's too big to put in a cupboard.

A. This is a waste of time.

B. Just keep feeling. We'll find it. *(At this point B is close to the corpse, near its feet. Silence as both feel in the dark, moving with great care. B touches C's right foot)* What the hell are you doing?

A. *(Now somewhere upstage centre, feeling their way across the back of the space)* What?

B. Get up. Stop messing about.

A. What?

B.   *(Realising voice is coming from 'wrong' direction)* Where are you?

A.   Over here, going clockwise.

B.   I've found a foot.

A.   What?

B.   *(Panicky. But keeping cool)* A foot. Someone's foot *(Feels further)* and leg. *(Pause)* There's someone in the bloody room.

A.   Where?

B.   Over here, somewhere in the middle.

A.   That's not funny.

B.   *(To C)* Hello? Are you awake?

A.   What the hell's going on?

B.   *(Vehemently)* Shut up will you. *(Silence as B feels up to C's right knee, then C's left knee and back down to the left foot)*

A.   *(Stands frozen in the darkness)* What are you doing?

B.   Shut up a minute. *(To C)* Hello? We're electricians – with the emergency services. There's been a power cut. Are you alright?

A.   Have you gone mad? What the hell are you talking about?

B.   *(To A)* Come over here. *(A moves towards B's voice. Both stretch out their hands)* Here, follow my voice.

A.   *(A is now standing over the corpse, arms stretched out, but doesn't touch it. Then they make contact with B's out-stretched arms)* There you are. What the hell's going on?

B.   *(Takes A's hands and places them on C's left knee, the knee closest to A. Silence)*

A.   *(Fairly loudly)* Jesus! Who's that?

B.   Shut up will you. Wait there. *(B moves up the body and slowly and carefully places hands on the corpse's* stomach. *Touches the cold, clasped hands)* It's a body. It's a bloody dead body.

A.   *(Finds an ankle)* Fuck.

B.   Shut up.

A.   *(At this stage, opposite B, on the other side of the table)* Let's get out of here – now.

B.   *(Instantly. Determined)* No. Look under the table.

A.   For God's sake.

B.   Look under the table. Get down and look. We'll both look. Come on. Get down. *(They both bend down to search under the table. A and B stretch out their arms and feel under the table. As this goes on C, the corpse, gets up slowly and stands at the upstage end of the table, facing the auditorium)*

A.   *(Stands)* I'm going. *(Without thinking, puts one hand on the table. Feels about where corpse should be)* O my God! *(Silence)*

B.   *(Just getting up. Angry with A's outburst)* What's wrong now? *(Silence)* Helloooo. What are you doing?

A.   It's gone.

B.   Funny. *(Sarcastically)*

A.   The bloody body's gone. *(C moves towards A and stands just a few centimetres away, then lifts a hand and touches A gently on the side of the face as A is just about to speak)* Let's get out of . . . *(Draws in breath. Freezes)*

B.   *(During the following B stands wondering what's going on. C moves round the table towards B)* What's wrong? *(Brief silence)* Where are you? *(Brief silence)* Speak, will you? *(Longer silence)* Who's there? Answer me for God's sake. *(C stands within centimetres of B)* Speak, will you?

5: Date

A. Hi.

B. Hi.

A. Were you looking for me?

B. Yeah, I was wondering . . .

A. You're looking for your book.

B. Yeah..I . . . no, not really.

A. I don't think you lent it to me.

B. No. Yeah. I know. Actually, I found it.

A. Oh good.
    (Pause)

B. Do you want to sit down?

A. Okay.

B. How's your day been?

A. Fine.

B. Can't wait for holidays.

A. Me neither. *(Pause)* I'd better watch the time. The bus.

B. Oh yeah.

A. Who had your book?

B. Found it at home, would you believe.

A. Actually, I must borrow it sometime.

B. Yeah, sure.
    (Pause)

A. Anyway . . .
    (Simultaneously)

B. I was wondering . . .

A. Sorry, go ahead.

B. No, go on.

A.   No, you wanted to ask me something.

B.   Yeah. *(Pause)* You see . . . I was wondering would you, would you like to go out with me sometime – to the cinema or for a meal or something.

A.   *(Unprepared)* Aaaaa . . . Yes. *(Brief pause)* Yeah.

B.   *(Expects A to say more)* Right. When? I mean there's no rush. You know, if you're studying and that.

A.   No, no. I mean yes. I am studying quite a bit but yes, I would like . . .

B.   Tomorrow evening?

A.   *(Brief pause)* Yeah, okay.

B.   Will I meet you here?

A.   Yeah, why not?

B.   Good, right.

A.   *(Getting up)* Oh, my bus. Must go.

B.   See you tomorrow then.

A.   *(Exiting)* Yeah, tomorrow.

B.   *(Remains sitting)* Bye.

6: Departure

A.　I'll see you then.

B.　Yeah, see you.

A.　Are you sure you know the way.

B.　Yeah, yeah, no problem.

A.　I'll go part of the way if you want.

B.　No, no, it's fine honestly.

A.　It's not that far you know.

B.　No, it's fine.

A.　Left after the traffic lights and then third on the right – okay?

B.　Yeah, I'll find it easily.

A.　Well, see you sometime – maybe Friday.

B.　Yeah, Friday, maybe Saturday. I must get going. Okay?

A.　Give us a call if you get lost.

B.　No, no.

A.　See you then.

B.　Yeah, and thanks for the help.

A.　No problem. You have my number don't you?

B.　Yeah, I have. Thanks. Bye.

A.　The shower seems to be passing. Could be a nice afternoon.

B.　Yeah – okay then. Cheers.

A.　You're not too late are you?

B.　No, no. See you *(Exiting)*

A.　*(Watches B exit)* See you then.

B.　*(Looks around to see A hasn't moved)* Bye. *(Exits)*

A.　Bye. *(Pause. Exit)*

7: Divided Space

A walks into the acting space with purpose. She surveys the space and walks it out. Cheerfully, she looks around. She steps out its width and breadth, counting carefully. She wants to find the halfway mark between stage right and left. This centre line is marked by A dragging her foot along the floor from up stage to down stage. Satisfied with the job, she goes off stage, gets two chairs and places one in the centre of each half, slightly more up stage than down stage.

A.   That's that, everything should be clear now. *(Takes a careful look around again, now taking in the auditorium for the first time. She takes a close, attentive look. As this is happening B arrives on stage from opposite wing to A)*

B.   Ah, you're here. *(Looks around)* So this is it?

A.   Yes, not bad is it?

B.   Not bad at all.

A.   Which side do you want? I'd like the left if you don't mind. The half way mark is about here I reckon. *(A walks line already 'marked' out by her)*

B.   What do you mean, left hand side?

A.   Which side do you want to act in?

B.   *(Surprised and puzzled)* I thought we were sharing the space?

A.   We are. You'll be on the right *(A moves to the right side of her divided space)* here, and *(moves to left side of divided space)* I'll be over here, on the left.

B.   *(Realises the point will have to be made more forcefully)* But I thought we were to use all the stage. *(While B says this he does a quick round doing his best to visit all the stage)*

A.   Oh, I see. Did you?

B.   There'll be more freedom.

A.   I don't think so. I'd prefer my own half. Separately, but simultaneously, if you see what I mean. More interesting.

B.   I don't think that's possible. There's only one stage. This is it. *(B's movement, by way of illustration, brings him to the centre of the stage right space)*

A.   *(Points to stage right)* Look. It's big enough.

B.   What do you mean? It's big enough.

A.   Your side of the stage. There's plenty of room for you.

B.   Look, you don't seem to understand. *(During the lines that follow, B creates movements to his words. Movement that, as far as he's concerned, demands the full space)* I need to move. To jump. To fall. To fly. To roll. To tumble. To travel through space .To run. To walk. To pace up and down. I mean how can we work together if we don't utilise the fuuuuuulllll *(Does a final run-around and stops with emphasis on)* space? *(This halt brings B close to A, who has been ignoring all the action. But A has had to get out of B's way once or twice. About half-way through B's exhibition A's demeanour and facial expression change distinctly. This should be clear to an audience. She is angry, determined)*

A.   *(A straight-arm point)* Please go over to your own side and then we'll talk about this.

B.   No, I don't think so.

      (Pause)

A.   *(In an instant A pushes B from behind and sends him over to the right hand side of the stage. In the process, B stumbles and falls. He gets up and dusts himself off. A is now just inside her side of the imaginary line that divides the two spaces, on guard, ready to protect her territory. Firm but calm)* The dividing line is here – as I said.

B. *(Still a little shocked. He doesn't move. Tries to remain calm and dignified)* I think – and feel – we should work with the full stage. So, I'm coming back.

A. I wouldn't advise that.

(Pause, then B takes a run at A to get into the other half. A manages to push B back. B falls again, gets up, brushes himself off)

A. I told you. Now, shall we start work?

B. No. *(Pause. B thinks about trying again but doesn't)* Tell me this.

A. What?

B. What right have you to half a stage?

A. The same right as you.

B. I don't want half a stage.

A. I don't want a full one – with you.

B. You agreed to work together.

A. Yes, of course.

B. Well?

A. We'll work together, simultaneously, independently. It's more original. You have your space and independence and I have mine.

B. I don't think I can tolerate this.

A. Well then, go. *(Before A has finished, B takes a run and falls and rolls into the middle of A's space)*

B. Gotcha.

A. *(Expressionless, A moves away from her proximity to B, but not into B's space)* That wasn't a wise move.

B. *(Rubbing a knee)* Perhaps not. But it was quick.

A. You've crossed the line again.

B. There is no line. The line's in your head.

A.   I want you to return to your space, please. Otherwise, we can't work.

B.   Not true.

(Pause)

A.   Well then. *(A goes over to B, who at this stage sits Indian style on the floor. She catches him under the arms and drags him across the line to the 'other side'. She then returns to the left side, finding a spot just inside the imagined line, half way between the rear and the front of the space. Exasperated)* Now, do you want to work?

B.   Of course I want to work, that's why I'm here, but a stage is a stage.

A.   Co-operation is sharing. We're sharing. Your half. My half.

B.   I want to work on *the* stage, not half the stage. I'll co-operate on a full stage. Anything else is nonsense. *(B gets to his feet and walks to what is now a clearly defined border, very close to, and facing A)* The line is in your head.

A.   *You* have no imagination. Two spaces are better than one. Who says one space is best?

B.   You're making a barrier. *(Pointing)* There's only one auditorium.

A.   *(Laughs off the logic)* Who says? *(B is about to respond but A continues)* One auditorium, one stage *(B waiting for catch)* but two spaces – do you hear me? – two creative spaces. It's original.

B.   You haven't a clue have you.

A.   That's your view. Actually, your problem is that I do have a view. I have a view of a drama to be played out by *you*, there, and *me*, here, in our own space, simultaneously, as I keep on saying.

B.   My drama is for the full stage. And by the way, you're included in it. You're part of it.

A. I don't want to be part of your – *drama.* My drama is that your drama – which, by the way, you don't need me for –*and* my drama will co-exist, side by side. Do you understand that?

B. *(Goes to cross the line. There's a brief pause, then some pushing and shoving. This should be carefully choreographed. B ends up well into A's space, lying down, feet facing the auditorium)* See. I'm here. It's a full stage, for everyone.

A. *(Considering B's vulnerable position)* I could get really violent.

B. *(Gets up quickly)* So could I. *(Pause. Slowly and consciously and with satisfaction, he walks over and back, the full width of the stage space. He stops centre and mid stage. He looks straight into the auditorium. He speaks calmly to the audience)* There is no line. There is no divide. There is a stage. *(Turns and points at A)* You are mistaken.

A. You're a stick in the mud. My drama will please the crowds. It will be different. In it, there's freedom for you, even you, and freedom for me. Artistic freedom. *(Pause)* And, by the way, I think you're a bit of a bully.

B. *Your* drama, *your* creation. You're the bully.

A. Would you mind moving into your space. We'll get somewhere then. *(B strides out the full width of the stage. Stops close to A. Pause)* Please go away.

B. Why don't you like me?

A. That's not the issue. The issue is the dramatic work we're here to create.

B. I agree.

A. You agree?

B. No drama yet though, because you've destroyed the space.

A.   Don't exaggerate. You want to commandeer the whole lot.

B.   *(Pause. Pointing to right side of stage)* You can move over there if you want.

A.   That's not funny.

B.   Wasn't meant to be.

A.   I don't want . . . look, I can *(She does this in B's right hand space)* gesticulate, declaim, strut in this space or that space. But it must be my own space. And I want you to have yours.

B.   Really? Well I'm happy to have you gesticulate, declaim, strut on the whole stage. You'd cramp my style. I need the whole stage.

A.   Just move into your space and we'll talk about it. *(A returns to her original space, the left, and stands beside B who at this stage is in A's chair)*

B.   I'm not going to do that. Why don't you give me an idea, for both of us? I'm willing to listen.

A.   Not while you're here.

      (Silence. No one moves)

B.   Give me one of your dramatic ideas and I'll move.

A.   No.

B.   Well, I'm not moving. *(Silence. A returns to B's space. B sees what she's about and gets up to follow)*

A.   *(Almost a scream)* Stay where you are or else! *(B freezes, just at the border)*

      (Slight pause)

B.   Are you threatening me?

A.   Why don't you sit down *(Pointing at chair in left space)* there.

B.   And you?

A.   I'll sit down – here. *(Sits)*

B. *(Pause. Thinks this might lead somewhere)* Right.

A. Right.

(Silence)

B. *(Looks over at A)* Is this your idea?

(Silence)

A. Could be.

(Silence)

B. What next?

(Silence)

A. When I say 'GO' we'll swap chairs as quickly as humanly possible. Then, we'll sit calmly until the next move.

B. And I'll give the next move. – I see.

A. *(Hardly lets B finish. Loudly)* Go! *(They swap seats as if trying to win a seat swapping competition. Each sits statue-like for a few seconds)* See.

B. See what?

A. See what I mean.

B. What do you mean?

A. Simultaneously independently.

B. No.

A. This is my space. That's yours.

B. You're impossible. *(Quite suddenly B gets up and rushes around frantically doing his best to go everywhere in the full space, weaving in and out of imaginary obstacles, chanting)* One space, one space, one space, one space, one space . . . *(This goes on for quite a while. Exhausted, B flops into the chair he got up from. Breathless and more to himself)* That was fun. *(To A)* Would you like to join in?

A. No.

B.   *(Changing tactics)* Ah, go on. Why not? It's easy. *(Gets up and does a shorter version, chanting his mantra)*

A.   I can do that. *(A jumps up and does her version of B's display, in the confines of half the stage, chanting her own mantra)* My space, my space, my space.

B.   *(When A returns to her seat)* Use the whole floor. Be my guest. By the way, that was my idea.

A.   So? Your idea. My space.

      (Long pause)

B.   This is going . . .

      (Together)

A.   This is going . . .

A.   Sorry, you go . . .

      (Together)

B.   Sorry, you go . . .

A.   No, it's okay.

      (Together)

B.   No, it's okay. No, go ahead.

A.   No, you do.

      (Pause)

B.   I was about to say . . .

      (Together)

A.   I was about to say . . .

B.   Just go ahead.

A.   Okay. I have a problem.

B.   Just what I was about to say.

A.   Solution?

B.   In your hands?

A.   *(Shakes head)* Not true.

B. Yes true. *(Pause. B gets up, lifts his chair to the centre of the stage, straddling the imaginary line. Sits)*

A. That means nothing. I'm not going away.

B. Neither am I.

A. Neither am I.

   (They sit on)

8: Filling Time

The lines suggested below are to encourage improvisation with action, and to produce successful sketches, or sketches that have the potential to be developed further. The object is to 'fill' two or three minutes of gesture, action or/and non-action around each set of lines – one for A and one for B. Of course, lines can come at any moment in the action and do not have to be delivered consecutively. What's written below should be regarded as suggestions only:

1. A. That's settled then.

    B. Suppose so.

2. A. And time goes so slowly.

    B. Don't annoy me.

3. A. I find this hard to believe.

    B. Believe me – it's true.

4. A. Well, what did/do you think of that?

    B. Wonderful. Truly. Wonderful.

5. A. Say something then!

    B. Cretin!

6. A. What's next?

    B. Wait. Wait.

7. A. I will.

    B. God, you're a gem.

8. A. Mad as a bloody hatter!

    B. Is there anybody there?

9. A. Excuse me – who are you?

    B. Me? Guess.

10. A. Lovely. Beautiful. Exquisite.

    B. Mmmmmm . . . whatever you say.

11. A.   I'm dying.
     B.   Everything will be fine – don't worry.
12. A.   It's for you.
     B.   No, no, no, no!
13. A.   You'll regret everything.
     B.   I'm sorry to have to do this.
14. A.   I can't see a thing.
     B.   Shhhh – it's too late.
15. A.   Sorry.
     B.   Sorry.

9: The Fitting Cubicle

A and B are in a clothes shop. The scene begins with B about to go into the fitting cubicle. This is an imaginary space about a metre square down stage right, but not right at the corner of the space. The imaginary cubicle might be marked out by masking tape. Its entrance is on the up stage side of the square. On the down stage side of the cubicle, inside, is an imaginary mirror. During the dialogue, when B is in the cubicle, A and B obviously can't see each other. The audience sees everything.

B is a reluctant shopper but has to do this because of some special occasion. A likes the shopping experience. Both take up positions before the scene begins, somewhere centre stage. The dressing and undressing done by B can be mimed. There is also a mirror in the shop 'hanging' on the down stage, auditorium wall.

A.   *(Handing B a garment)* This one first, then this. Go on.

B.   *(Moving towards cubicle)* This wearies me.

A.   Go on, go on – make an effort will you?

B.   *(In cubicle. Only now looking at garments)* The blue's okay, isn't it?

A.   *(Shouts in)* It's lovely. I'd say it'll be stunning. Well, is it on?

B.   *(Struggles with taking off and putting on garment)* Will you wait! *(B emerges wearing garment. Not convinced)*

A.   Stand back there. Let me see. Fabulous! Wonderful!

B.   *(Walks around a little. Looks in mirror)* No, don't like it. *(Pause)*

A.   Okay. Try the green one anyway.

(B enters the cubicle and changes again. A, meanwhile, scans the imaginary shelves of the shop looking for something more adventurous for B and finds it. This

garment is a little more difficult to get on and off. A takes it and goes to the cubicle entrance and without looking in, hands the garment to B)

B. You can't be serious!

A. *(Shouts in)* Try it on will you. Let's have a look. Come out and let me see the green first.

B. *(B appears from cubicle. Walks across the shop floor)* No, no, no – a waste of time. *(Returns to cubicle)*

A. Whatever you say. Now try that red and green thing. It's dead on – very special.

B. *(In cubicle. Looks at the 'very special' garment)* You're serious, aren't you?

A. Go on, try it. It's different.

B. *(In cubicle. Goes through the process of removing and putting on)* This is crazy. I won't be wearing this, I can tell you.

A. *(To B as they put it on and adjust it before coming out)* Just put it on and let me have a look.

B. Yeah but . . .

A. *(During this speech B is in the cubicle)* When it comes to style be bold – that's my motto. I've advised you well in the past, haven't I? So stop grumbling. *(B emerges from cubicle. Stands listening to A who continues to browse)* Why you find shopping for clothes so hard I'll never understand. Anyway, we'll get something stunning for you today – I feel it. *(A turns. Suppresses shock at what is clearly a bad call)* Wow, wow, wow. Different.

B. But?

A. *(Walks around B. Perversely, holds to the initial enthusiasm)* No, no. No buts. *(Slight pause)* You'll cut a dash in that I can tell you.

B. *(Steps towards shop mirror)* But does it look good on me? Do you like it?

A.   *(Avoids questions)* Makes you look younger – yes, younger.

B.   *(Warming to the 'the look')* Yeah?

A.   And more confidant.

B.   Really?

A.   Yeah, really. I told you. Trust me. *(Looks at B, looking in mirror. Very uncertain)* What do you think?

B.   Yeah, I like it. I think it's good. Do you think I need the bigger size? *(Another look in mirror)* Yeah, I'll try the bigger size anyway. Wait there. *(Exits, calling shop assistant)* Excuse me? Excuse me?

10: Fruit in a Suitcase

Two characters, A and B, are on stage – half facing each other and half facing the audience, with a table between them. A, at stage right, looks up and out into the auditorium and B, to their left, looks down and out in front. There is silence for quite a while.

A.   *(Looks over at B. Long pause)* Peaches, tomatoes, mandarins, bananas and a large melon.

B.   And cucumbers. Don't forget the cucumbers. *(Long pause)*

A.   Why?

B.   How should I know?

A.   Nothing else?

B.   Nothing.

A.   What will we do?

B.   Ask him straight. Where are your clothes? Why is the suitcase full of fruit?

A.   I think we'll leave it. There could be a perfectly reasonable explanation.

B.   It's a present – to us!

A.   Don't be daft. *(At this point C enters)*

11: **Ghost Presence**

A and B are dating. B has met and fallen in love with C. C's presence on stage is as a spirit, a jealous one, invisible to both A and B. Only the audience hears C. A and B are in a restaurant about to have a meal. They sit either side of a small table. C stands at B's shoulder and sometimes moves to the up stage side of the table.

A.　*(Intimate silence)* This is lovely isn't it?

B.　Yes. Thanks for the treat.

A.　Penny for your thoughts.

B.　Oh, nothing much really.

C.　Liar.

A.　You must be thinking of something.

B.　Ummmh . . . let me see.

C.　You're thinking about me, aren't you? About us.

B.　Not really. *(Pause)* I think I was thinking about the last time we were out.

A.　We went for a dive by the lake and came here after.

B.　Did we? Was that the last time?

A.　Yeah, remember – it was too cold to swim.

B.　Oh yes – that's all really.

A.　What place were you thinking of?

B.　Can't remember really – that lovely guest house a while back.

A.　You're just shy, that's all, isn't it?

C.　You're not shy with me, are you?

B.　No, no, not me.

A.　Okay, tell me what you're really thinking.

B.　Haven't the foggiest really. *(Looks around)* I was thinking about the odd décor of this place.

C.   Or when you were with me – you gorgeous thing.

A.   *(Sees B smiling)* Mmmm . . . smiling now.

C.   *(Snaps to A)* Bloody nosey parker. You're a gonner, mate, you know that.

A.   Anyway, what are you going to have?

C.   You'll have the fish. I introduced you to that – over there at the corner table.

B.   The fish I think – for a change.

A.   Fish, really?

B.   I hear it's really good.

A.   That's a first.

B.   Yeah, someone I know was here recently and said it was really good. You having pasta?

C.   Someone you know – intimately.

A.   You're strange.

C.   *(To A)* You're an idiot.

B.   No, no, just a change of mates – I mean tastes. Being adventurous and all that.

A.   You just said 'mates' – now I know what's on your mind.

B.   *(Laughs)* Did I? Yeah, strange. Caught out there, I suppose.

C.   'Mates' – that's us, isn't it? 'Mates' with tastes.

B.   Funny that, 'mates' and 'tastes'. *(Pause)*

A.   Oh, how's that noisy ground-floor neighbour of yours? Have you seen her since?

B.   Yeah, once or twice, coming and going.

A.   Really?

B.   Yeah, yeah. Things have quietened down there for some reason. Now, let's see, what else is on tonight?

12: **Hi and Bye**

A. Hi.

B. Hi.

A. You well?

B. Fine, and you?

A. Fine.

B. Good.

A. What's happening?

B. Yeah, what's happening?

A. Not much.

B. No, nothing much.

A. Must go –see you later.

B. Me too – see you then.

13: In Love

A.   *(Walks on. Is obviously very happy. To audience, in confidence)* Have you ever been in love? I'm in love you know. I am, seriously. It's wonderful.

B.   *(Calls from off-stage)* I'm here. *(B is friendly, business-like, but not at all intimate. It is obvious that B hasn't considered A romantically in the slightest)* Hi. Here's the letter. Haven't a clue how it ended up in my bag.

A.   *(Fussed and nervous. Doing their best to contain excitement)* Won't you stay for a coffee?

B.   I can't really – must rush.

A.   Kettle's on. It won't be a minute. Sit down there.

B.   No, honestly I can't.

A.   Oh, go on. *(Thinking quickly)* In fact there's something I wanted to ask you *(More quick thinking)* about the play . . . yeah, the . . . ah . . . there's a bit I haven't a clue about.

14: Pigs and Insurance

Through movement, facial expression, tone of voice and character, A should express a sense of repressed disgust and discomfiture at their situation. Character B is totally oblivious to this. The scene is a farm. A is an insurance salesperson. The location is the pigsty where A finds B in a pen with a sow and the piglets, all imagined. The insurance person A stands on the edge, doing their best to ensure that B renews the premium. What's important is the smell, the muck under his feet and dirty surroundings – all imagined.

A. *(Enters while B, already on stage, in an imaginary pen, is doing all the actions that suggest working with pigs – feeding, checking ears, examining)* Ah, I thought I'd find you here. How are things with you, Farmer?

B. Oh, it's yourself. I was looking out for you.

A. They're fine looking pigs.

B. Indeed they are. She's produced a grand litter. Look at this fellow. *(B walks to edge of pen, holding out a piglet for A to take. A has to find somewhere relatively clean to put down his imaginary briefcase)* Isn't he lovely?

A. Lovely. *(A holds piglet awkwardly, considers it for a moment; hands it back)*

B. Do you think we're in for a dry spell? It'll dry up all this muck. I hope you didn't get too dirty coming down here.

A. Ah, no. Not too bad.

B. Have you seen this new pig feed? Funny old stuff.

A. *(B hands A some of the animal feed. A does their best to feel the texture and look interested)* I see what you mean.

B. Would you step in here and give me a hand with this plank like a good man (woman).

A. *(Steps over dirty fence, doing his best not to touch anything that might ruin his suit. A and B then proceed to lift and carry an imaginary, manure-caked plank)* You have those little fellows well looked after.

B. Oh, indeed I do. Are you right there? That'll do you. We'll drop it here. *(B drops the plank and some sludge skits up. B is unaware of the splatter that ends up on A's suit. Sees him looking at his clothes)* Alright there? We'll go up to the house now and settle our business.

A. *(Steps in some manure. Almost given up on their efforts)* Fine, fine.

B. Oh, will you take this mucky little fellow with you up to the house for me? He's a bit sick looking – will you manage there?

A. *(Forced cheerfulness. Takes sick piglet)* No problem.

B. Good, good. Go ahead there. I'll follow you up and we'll have a cup of tea. Hold him tight now. He's a lively little fellow. *(Exit A followed by B)*

15: Promise

A.   Now. Now. Now. I want it now. A promise is a promise.

B.   *(Pause)* Tomorrow.

A.   Are you serious? *(Pause. No response from B)* Don't worry, you said. No problem, you said. Mum's the word. Well it's not fair.

B.   *(Interrupts)* Hold it – would you listen. Just listen.

A.   I'm listening. *(Pause)*

B.   Look. You've already waited. *(Brief pause)* What's another night?

A.   *(Cuts in)* Because you said! Didn't you? Go on, admit it. You said.

B.   Yeah – okay, I did. But . . .

A.   *(A little frantic)* But, but, but, but . . . *(Angry)* No buts. Tomorrow. Okay? *(Pause)* Say it to me. *(Pause)* Go on, say it! TO-MOR-O. *(Pause)*

B.   Tomorrow.

A.   And again. *(Pause)* Go on.

B.   Tomorrow.

A.   Right. That's settled. See you tomorrow. *(Exit)*

B.   *(Gets up to follow)* I'll do my best.

16: Tell Me

Two characters. Two chairs. Throughout the conversation B remains silent but reacts with a number of clear but subtle gestures. During A's questioning they might get up and move around. Numerous pauses should be introduced to allow for gesture, eye contact, thought.

A. Go on, please, tell me. Honestly, I won't say a word. I won't say anything. What difference will it make? Just the bare facts. I won't say a word. I promise– big time. Anyway, who cares whether I know or not? Please. I'm not involved. Please, please, please. Go on, please.

17: **Visit from Shakespeare**

*A sits in a chair, downstage right, facing the auditorium.
There is an empty chair about two metres away and to the
left of A. It also faces the auditorium. A is reading or perhaps
just thinking. They remain unaware as B enters from stage
left and sits on the vacant chair. B is a ghost. The ghost
smiles and looks out into the audience.*

A. *(Suddenly noticing B in their peripheral vision, A jumps
    out of the chair)* Holy shite! *(A's mouth is open; eyes
    fixed on B, the ghost)* Who are you? *(Pause. No
    immediate reaction from B who slowly turns to look at A,
    continuing to smile)*

B. Shakespeare. Will Shakespeare, poet and dramatist.

A. You're joking.

B. I jest not.

A. *(Uncertainly)* William Shakespeare – the fellow who wrote
    Hamlet?

B. The very same, sir. And you?

A. Me?

B. Pray tell, who are you?

A. I'm . . . . *(Gives name. The ghost gets up to go. A watches
    for a moment)* Stay, stay, please. *(The ghost calmly stops
    mid movement, freezes for an instant and returns to
    their seat. A looks right and then left beyond the ghost
    and into audience)* Can I ask you a few questions, *(Pause)*
    Sir?

B. Prithee, friend, let me guess. *(Smugly)* Something
    concerning the Lord Hamlet?

A. Yeah, yeah, how did you guess?

B. Studying under dim light, my tragedy, Hamlet, Prince of
    Denmark. I have watched thee.

A. Really?

B. Prithee, tell me what doest thou need to know. My speech shall please thee well before I go.

A. Boy, I don't know where to begin. Let me see. *(Pause)* Right, first question: Were Hamlet and Ophelia having sex – were they?

18: When to Move

In this scene A has to find the most appropriate and natural moment in the conversation, before the end, to move physically across the room to sit beside B, without seeming creepy, overly presumptuous or flirtatious. Of course, at some point in the exchange we may also see A 'move' mentally or even emotionally – a different moment from their movement across stage. A and B, a boy and girl, are both in their twenties. They only know each other by sight and each hasn't paid much attention to the other. Both have chosen a college module on 'The Art and History of Popular Song.' The space is set up like a waiting room. Perhaps two row of chairs facing each other but in chevron formation, opening out toward audience. A, the boy, is already seated in one row, reading. Both carry papers and perhaps a book.

B. *(Enters. Sits in row opposite. B looks up at A briefly catching his eye as he glances up also)* Hi.

A. (Smiles) Hi.

B. *(Long pause and silence. Takes out book or papers. Begins to concentrate. A looks up again and quickly studies B, who remains unaware)*

A. *(Returns to papers for a moment and looks up again. Pause)* Did you manage to get a copy of the lyric?

B. Pardon?

A. The words of the song. Did you get a copy for the presentation?

B. Yes, eventually.

A. It's good – I like it.

B. Well, I haven't really looked, – it's all a bit rushed. *(Pause. Returns to work. Without looking up)* It's full of references to other songs apparently.

A. *(Pause. Watches B reading for a very short moment. Holds up a sheet of paper)* I found a very good website with all that stuff on it. You didn't come across it?

B. *(Half looking up)* No, I'm just reading it now – the song. Busy week.

A. Oh, sorry. I'll leave you to it. *(A resumes reading for a few seconds. Looks up at B again who is concentrating. Goes back to his work briefly and looks up again. Long silence)*

B. *(Looks up. Almost catches A looking)* Ten minutes isn't it.

A. *(Feigns not hearing properly)* Sorry?

B. Each of us has to speak for ten minutes.

A. Yeah, that's right.

B. A 'Chevy' is a car isn't it?

A. Yeah, he drove his 'Chevy to the levee / But the levee was dry'. Where all the cool young people hung out, I presume.

B. *(Returns to preparation)* Yeah, I guess.

A. *(Resumes work. Looks at watch. Long pause)* I'm sure you'll be fine.

B. *(Without looking up)* We'll see. *(Pause, suddenly)* Oh, what time is it? We're not late are we?

A. No, no – about five minutes.

B. Is Jack Flash a reference to the Rolling Stones?

A. Yeah, so it seems.

B. *(Reading)* Right. *(Forgetting)* Oh thanks. *(Pause. Stands up. Goes to exit)* I think I'll go in. Thanks for that and all the best yourself.

A. *(Instinctively stands. Unsure what to do next)* Not at all, that's fine. *(B exits. Although they're going to the same place, A doesn't move)*

19: You do Love Me

A. You love me, don't you?

B. Yes, I love you.

A. You've always loved me, haven't you?

B. Yes, of course. I've always loved you.

A. *(Almost cuts off B)* No second thoughts?

B. No, of course not.

A. Never?

B. Never.

A. And for ever and ever?

B. For ever and ever.

A. 'till death do us . . .?

B. 'till death do us. *(Pause)* For better or worse.

A. Really?

B. Really.

A. Never a flicker?

B. A flicker?

A. Of doubt.

B. No.

A. Regrets?

B. Regrets?

A. Yes, regrets.

B. *(Pause)* I love you.

A. You love me. That makes me feel good. Do you feel good?

B. Yes – I love you.

A. Yeah, I feel good.
    (Both exit)

20: **Dead Dog**

A and B (with newspaper) are strangers sitting at the same table in a coffee shop. A can be an elderly woman or man. B is a middle-aged person of either gender. For a while both are in their own separate worlds but the elderly A is a little agitated and upset. B gradually becomes aware of this before A speaks.

A.   *(Stares at B for a while before speaking)* Excuse me?

B.   Yes.

A.   I wonder would you be able to help me?

B.   *(Cautiously)* Yes?

A.   My dog died.

B.   Oh dear, I'm sorry to hear that. *(Attempts to return to coffee and newspaper)*

A.   Yes. He died this morning.

B.   *(Looks up)* Really. *(Tries again to return to newspaper)* *(Pause)*

A.   Could you help me?

B.   *(Trying to keep it vague)* Sorry?

A.   Would you be able to help me? *(Looks straight at B)* I'd be very . . . . . . grateful.

B.   *(Before speaking, he looks around the coffee shop to see if anyone's listening)* I'm not sure. I have to go very soon.

A.   This won't take a minute. You see Rex died in the living room and I'm on the fourth floor over there *(Pointing into auditorium)* and I can't get him down. *(Brief pause)* I want to get him into the back garden where I have a lovely plot for him you see – under the old apple tree. *(Long pause)* It wouldn't take you long at all. I can see you're a kind person. *(Pause)* Please will you come with me now?

21: Strange Meeting

A and B remain standing for the entire scene.

A.   *(Walks on stage. Preoccupied. Worried. They are waiting for someone. Looks around as they wait. Looks at watch)*

B.   *(Enters unnoticed by A)* Hello.

A.   *(Turns. Uncertain)* Hello.

B.   Waiting long?

A.   *(Assumes this is the person)* No, no. Not long. It's okay.

B.   Was it a calm crossing?

A.   Very, yes. It's a lovely day.
     (Pause)

B.   You finally made it. It's good of you to come. *(Pause)* Did you tell her?

A.   *(Shakes head)* I feel I should have.

B.   Do they ever mention me?

A.   Shall we sit somewhere?

B.   Yes of course. Would you like to walk along the pier or go for a drink?

A.   I don't mind really – a drink perhaps.

B.   Yes, okay. We'll find a quiet place. *(Pause)* You probably know the whole story at this stage.

A.   I'm not so sure. *(Pause)* Do you know somewhere quiet?

B.   Yes, yes, I do. It's not far.
     (Both exit)

22: **Ways of Dying**

*A bench with a back on it or three or four chairs side by side,
facing the auditorium, are needed for this script. There are
three characters, A, B and C, and a newspaper. A enters,
relaxed, sees newspaper on the bench and looks pleased.
They sit down to read it. A scans the paper and settles on the
Death notices.*

A.   *(Reads)* Oldham-Murray, Sinkerstown, Ballyduff, April 6th
     at 6.00pm. *(Peacefully)* In the loving care of . . . *(A stops.
     Considers)*
     Peacefully *(Continues with silent reading for a few
     moments)* Tracey Applehouse, Tinoakley, April 5th at
     8.30pm. *(Peacefully)* Jenny, beloved of Connie and dearly
     loved father . . . *(Stops. Considers)* Peacefully.
     Peacefully. *(Smiles calmly. Dies)*

B.   *(Enters. Glances at A while walking past and sees that
     they are 'snoozing'. Seeing the newspaper they decide to
     sit at the other end of the bench. Delicately, they slowly
     take the newspaper from A and begin to scan the pages.
     After a few moments, they settle on the Death notices.
     Reads)* Thorn, Arkdale, Castlecairn, April 5th at 9.30pm.
     Suddenly at home. Beloved of Mary and Jonathan. *(Stops.
     Considers)* Suddenly. *(Reads again)* Thornton, nee Smith,
     April 5th at Midnight. Suddenly. Sadly missed. *(Stops.
     Considers)* Suddenly. Mmmmm . . . Suddenly. *(Pause. Dies
     suddenly)*

C.   *(Enters and walks across the acting space behind bench.
     Sees the two 'sleeping'. Spots the newspaper, looks
     around and, slowly, with expert care, extracts
     newspaper from B's grip. They fold it up, look around
     and walk off)*

23: **Where Are You Going?**

A and B walk across the acting space from either wing. They are complete strangers.

A. *(Approaches B)* Excuse me, where are you going?

B. What do you mean, where am I going?

A. Where are you off to, right now?

B. Is this a survey or something?

A. No, no. I'd just like to know where you're going.

B. I don't understand.

A. I'm curious as to where you're going.

B. It's none of your business where I'm going.

A. I'm only asking.

B. Well don't ask. Who the hell are you anyway?

A. Just a nice person taking an interest in where you're going.

B. Look, are you trying to be funny.

A. No, I told you. I'm just curious about where you're going.

B. *(Makes move to go)* It's none of your business where I'm going.

A. *(Blocks B's path)* Okay, just gimmie a clue.

B. *(Angrily)* I told you – just go away.

A. *(Rapidly)* If I guess will you tell me if I'm right?

B. *(Looks around)* Go-a-way!

A. You're being very unreasonable you know.

B. *(Makes another move to go)* Just piss off will you?

A. *(Blocks B again)* The Tax Office. That's it. You're going to the Tax Office, aren't you?

B. No, I'm not going to the . . . look would you get out of my way.

A.   The library? Just nod if I'm right.

B.   Get out of my way.

A.   Yes, I'm right. It's the library. You're going to the library.

B.   I'm going to hit you if you don't get out of my way – do you hear me? *(A jumps back)* Bloody lunatic. *(Manages to get past A. Storms off)*

A.   *(Shouts after B)* No need to get violent *(Pause)* Spoil sport.

24: The Sandwich

B is on a diet. A has a bet with B about not eating between meals. C is sympathetic to B's efforts.

The furniture is a table and two chairs. Everything else in the kitchen – fridge, cupboard etc. – is imagined.

(It's about 2am in the morning. B appears, slowly, silently. It's dark. B, ravenous, could murder for a toasted sandwich. B goes through the routine of making the sandwich. Now and then they freeze, thinking that A might appear. C, unheard by B, approaches. As C slowly enters, B exits at opposite wing to get a drink. C sees the sandwich. Wonders. Sits down and eats sandwich, then exits. B re-enters. Goes for sandwich. Baffled. Starts the process all over again)

A.   *(Calls from off)* Anyone there? *(B abandons sandwich making. Hides behind imaginary fridge)* Hello? Who's there? *(Pause)* I'm coming in! *(A enters. Looks around. Calls out C's first name and then B's)* Who's up? *(Sees abandoned sandwich making. Looks around again. Goes to leave. Thinks again. Sits down to eat sandwich. B comes out from hiding and tiptoes off)*

25a: **Lost in Translation**

The scene takes place in a small, family-run filling station deep in the heart of rural France. Character A is looking for the house of an old colleague. He has almost no French.

A. Hello – do you speak English?

B. Pardon?

A. Sorry. *(Very self-conscious)* Do you speak English?

B. No, No, Not at all.

A. I'm looking for the Gelineaus – the Gelineau's house. Henry and Agnes. Somewhere near here.

B. Sorry, I don't understand. *(Points at A)* You are Mr Gelineau?

A. *(Hears question in tone)* No, no, I'm not Mr Gelineau. *(Points, gestures)* Outside, around village – the Gelineaus. Big tall man, long hair.

B. Sorry, I don't understand.

A. The address has the word, 'Lakeside'.

B. *(Recognises the name of a restaurant)* Ah, the restaurant. *(Mimics eating)* Oh, yes. Straight for about ten kilometres, and then left. *(Pointing)*

A. No, no, not a restaurant. *(Mimes walls and roof)* House, house.

B. *(Puzzled. Still sees a picture of a restaurant in A's mime)* Yes, yes, ten kilometres and then left, left.

A. *(To himself)* No, I don't think so. *(To B)* The Gelineau family.

B. *(Faint recognition of word)* Family?

A. *(Onto something)* Yes, yes, the family, Gelineau.

B. *(Trying to repeat A's pronunciation and accent syllable by syllable)* Gel – in – o.

A.   *(Despair)* Yes, Gelineau, somewhere around here, in the country.

B.   *(Sudden dawning. Quickly, in a rush of enthusiasm)* Ah, yes Gelineau. Yes, yes, Henry and Agnes. Left at roundabout and five kilometres and then left and then right at the small white cross at the crossroads at the sunflower field. *(B, very happy with themselves, stands and smiles broadly at A)*

A.   *(A is baffled by the speed of the instructions. To B, as if English will be perfectly understood)* Now, let's start again, shall we?

25b: Lost in Translation (French)

The scene takes place in a small, family-run filling station deep in the heart of rural France. Character A is looking for the house of an old colleague. He has almost no French.

A. **Bonjour.** Do you speak English?

B. **Pardon?**

A. Sorry. *(Very self-conscious)* **Parlez-vous** English?

B. **Non. Non. Pas du tout.**

A. I'm looking for the Gelineaus – the Gelineau's house. Henry and Agnes. Somewhere near here.

B. **Pardon, je ne comprends pas.** *(Points at A)* **Vous vous appelez 'Gelineau'?**

A. *(Hears the question in tone)* No, no. I'm not Mr Gelineau. *(Points, gestures)* Outside, around the village – the Gelineaus. Big tall man, long hair.

B. **Je suis désolé. Je ne comprends pas.**

A. The address has the word 'Lakeside'.

B. *(Recognises the name of a restaurant)* **Ah, le restaurant!** *(Mimics eating)* **Ah, bon, oui! Tout droit pour dix kilomètres, et puis à gauche.** *(Pointing)*

A. No, no, not a restaurant. *(Mimes walls and roof)* House. House!

B. *(Puzzled. Still sees a picture of a restaurant in A's mime)* **Oui, oui, vous allez dix kilomètres et puis à gauche – à gauche.**

A. *(To himself)* No, I don't think so. *(To B)* The Gelineau family.

B. *(Faint recognition of word)* **Famille?**

A. *(Onto something)* Yes, yes, the Gelineau family . . .

B. *(Trying to repeat A's pronunciation and accent syllable by syllable)* Gel – in – o.

A.   *(Despair)* Yes. Gelineau, somewhere around here, in the country.

B.   *(Sudden dawning. Quickly, in a rush of enthusiasm)* **Ah, oui Gelineau! Oui, oui! Henri et Agnes. Vous tournez à gauche au rondpoint, vous continuez cinq kilomètres, tournez à gauche et puis à droite à la petite croix blanche au carrefour près du champ de tournesols.** *(B very happy with himself, stands and smiles broadly at A)*

A.   *(A is baffled by the speed of the instructions in French. To B, as if English will be perfectly understood)* Now, let's start again, shall we?

25c: Lost in Translation (Spanish)

The scene takes place in a small, family-run filling station deep in the heart of rural Spain. Character A is looking for the house of an old colleague. He has almost no Spanish.

A.   **Buenos días** do you speak English?

B.   **¿Perdone, Senor?**

A.   Sorry *(Very self-conscious)* **Habla** English?

B.   **No, lo siento, ni una palabra.**

A.   I'm looking for the Gelineaus – the Gelineau's house. Henry and Agnes. Somewhere near here.

B.   **Lo siento, no entiendo ¿Es usted El Señor Gelineau?**

A.   *(Hears question in tone)* No, no, I'm not Mr Gelineau. *(Points, gestures)* Outside, around village – the Gelineaus. Big tall man, long hair.

B.   **Lo siento Señor, no entiendo.**

A.   The address has the word, 'Lakeside'.

B.   *(Recognises the name of a restaurant)* **Ah, El restaurante** . . . *(Mimics eating)* **Sí, Sí Siga todo recto unos diez kilómetros y entonces tuerza a la izquierda.** *(Pointing)*

A.   No, no, not a restaurant. *(Mimes walls and roof)* House, house.

B.   *(Puzzled. Still sees a picture of a restaurant in A's mime)* Sí, Sí diez kilómetros y luego a la izquierda, la izquierda.

A.   *(To himself)* No, I don't think so. *(To B)* The Gelineau family.

B.   *(Faint recognition of word)* **¿Familia?**

A.   *(Onto something)* Yes, yes, the family, Gelineau.

B.   *(Trying to repeat A's pronunciation and accent syllable by syllable)* Gel – in – o

A.   *(Despair)* Yes, Gelineau, somewhere around here, in the country.

B.   *(Sudden dawning. Quickly, in a rush of enthusiasm)* **Ah Sí, Sí Gelineau, Sí, Enrique y Añes. Tuerza a la izquierda a la glorieta, siga unos cinco kilómetros y luego doble a la izquierda y entonces a la derecha a la pequeña cruz blanca al cruce donde hay el campo con los girasoles.** *(B, very happy with himself stands and smiles broadly at A)*

A.   *(A is baffled by the speed of the instructions in Spanish. To B, as if English will be perfectly understood)* Now, let's start again, shall we?

Note   If character A is female the word Señor should be replaced by Señora.

26: Afraid of the Dark

B is on stage alone. There is an empty chair beside her. B sits for a few moments in silence, then, quite deliberately, closes her eyes. Suddenly she shouts and opens her eyes. A comes running from offstage.

A. What's wrong?

B. I'm afraid of the dark.

A. It's not dark. In fact, it's a bright, sunny day.

B. *(Looks at A as if they are stupid)* I know that! I told you I'm afraid of the dark.

A. Oh.

B. It's not nice, the dark. The darkness.

A. Since when?

B. The last time I shut my eyes. It was terrifying.

A. *(Brief pause)* It's only the dark.

B. Easy for you to say.

A. Try again. Maybe it's gone.

B. It's always dark when you close your eyes.

A. I mean the fear. Shut them tight for a moment.

B. No, I can't.

A. Go on. I'm here.

B. Hold my hand.

A. Okay. Okay. *(A holds B's hand and looks at B, waiting. B braces herself before shutting her eyes firmly. There's a brief pause and B shouts with fright and opens her eyes. They become aware that the two of them are holding hands. B (or A) takes away their hand, perhaps with slight embarrassment)*

B. What'll I do?

A. *(Brief pause)* I have to go.

B.   *(With a touch of panic)* Don't. *(More controlled)* Please stay.

A.   I can't.

B.   What'll I do?

A.   *(Trying to be positive and cheerful)* Exhaustion will help. You'll get so tired you'll be asleep before you realise it. You won't notice the dark.

B.   Stay for a while, please.

A.   I can't, honestly. *(Stands)* I must go. Get yourself a good book.

B.   I won't. This is terrible.

A.   Terrifying, you mean. Sorry. Bad joke.

B.   Please . . .

A.   I'm going, okay. See you tomorrow. *(Almost off stage)* Get a good night's sleep. Bye. *(A exits, and a long silence follows, in which B does some serious thinking about her predicament. Then, she shuts her eyes for a second, cries out and opens them again. B looks around, worried)*

27: Murder in the Park

The scene is a public park. Arrange the chairs in the acting space close together in a row, as if they were a park bench. There are two strangers sitting on the park bench. It is important to note that the scene begins quite a while before A speaks. A could be reading a newspaper.

A.   It's a lovely day isn't it?

B.   *(Slight pause)* Yes, it is.

     (Silence)

A.   It's lovely to hear the children's voices. *(No response)* I say, it's lovely to hear the children's voices.

B.   *(Somewhat reluctantly)* Yes, it is. *(Silence)*

A.   Are you from around here?

B.   No, no.

A.   No, I didn't think you were.

B.   *(No response)*

A.   That was a terrible murder last week, wasn't it?

B.   Sorry?

A.   That was a terrible murder. Last week. Horrific.

B.   Sorry, I wasn't aware.

A.   Ah, you're better off. It was gruesome. The young man was strangled – just over there, by the trees.

B.   Really.

A.   Yes. With a green curtain cord would you believe.

B.   That's shocking. *(Pause)*

A.   They'll never find him. *(No response)* Not in a million years, will they? Awful.

     (Long Pause)

B.   You' re right you know.

A.   Pardon?

B.   You're right, I said. They'll probably never find him.

28: After Friel

Two players represent character A on stage. One is A Public and the other is A Private. The former, as the name suggests, is the outer face and voice of the character, the part that interacts with others, the part that is public. The latter, A Private, is the inner voice, the voice that no one hears, the voice that might sometimes be the public voice. A Private is invisible to all.

(A Public and A Private enter, stage right. A Private immediately goes to the rear of the space (upstage centre) and sits on a chair. A Public stands in the centre of the space. A Public looks around. There are two more chairs stage right. A Public goes and gets these and places them centre stage, facing each other and about a metre apart. A Public then stands back up-stage to consider the positioning of the chairs)

A Private. Too confrontational.

A Public. *(Returns to the chairs and re-positions them about two metres apart. Steps back to consider)*

A Private. Too big a gap, silly – too close to the truth.

A Public. *(Considers. Brings one chair in a bit, then the other. The distance apart is now somewhere in between position one and position two)* Mmmmmm.

A Private. Something not quite right here.

A Public. *(Considers again)* Make up your mind will you? *(Here, A's name might be used. Leaves the chairs the same distance apart – about one and a half metres – but turns each chair until it faces diagonally across to the front corner of the stage space, allowing for better sight lines)*

A Private. Better, better.

A Public.   *(Sits on this chair. A Public thinks about its direction and position. Considers the position of the other chair too. Without moving, he imagines vividly the person who will sit in the facing chair)* Are you talking to me, punk? *(Pause)*

A Private.   Honesty. Frankness. Go for it.

A Public.   *(To other chair)* Look, I love you. It's that simple.

A Private.   Easy, easy – don't gush it all out at once. What about timing?

A Public.   *(Gets up. Goes to the other chair and repositions it in the same way. It's on stage right so it now faces the downstage corner of stage left. Sits on it. Looks across at the other chair)* That's better.

A Private.   A stickler for the little detail. Maybe that's what caused the trouble in the first place?

A Public.   *(Gets up. Steps back. Considers. Closes gap a little between chairs)*

A Private.   Leave it, leave it. Not too much.

A Public.   *(Steps back again. Considers)*

A Private.   Just about right, eh? A little closer?

A Public.   *(Moves both chairs a fraction closer to each other)* Now.

A Private.   *(During the following, A Public paces the room, visiting both chairs to get the perspective of each, trying to get a sense of the anticipated conversation, objectively. As A Public moves around he takes on gestures appropriate to, and suggested by, A Private's lines)*

A Private.   Now, what to say? How to say it? The desired outcome . . . mmmm. Desire's the thing here, isn't it? Let's be honest. Anyway, don't exaggerate. Don't lie. You're a useless liar in this situation *(After-thought)*, in any situation. See both points of view – for a while. Don't just melt and give in. Some resistance is good. Be yourself. *(Pause)* Without the silly jokes, okay? Relax, relax – sit down will you. *(A Public sits on stage left chair, the one he intends to stay on)* It's not the end of the world – or is it? You'll be heartbroken, won't you? No, no. No negative thoughts. The signs are good. *(Pause. Silence. A Private looks at A Public. A Public reflects. Suddenly, A Public jumps up and moves, upstage away from chairs, as if they were alive. Freezes)* What the hell are you at? Are you mad? No, not mad. Stupid. Flight or face it –that's the question. Shhhh . . . too late, someone's coming. Sit down, you idiot. Look casual, composed. Get rid of that glum face.

A Public.   Hello. *(Calling towards off stage right)* Is that you? *(Supply name)* I'm here.

29: Serious Problem

A. Next please. *(B enters with a worried look)* Sit down there.

B. I can't . . .

A. Sorry?

B. I can't doctor – that's the problem.

A. What's the problem?

B. *(Quite upset)* You see doctor, every time I sit on a chair I fall off. I just can't help myself. I'm not in control.

A. Really?

B. Yes, it's terrible. I can't go anywhere. I just can't control it.

A. Mmmmm. Could you show me there? *(Reluctantly, slowly, B sits down. Pause. They lose control and fall off)*

B. *(Stands up. Worried)* You see doctor.

A. I see. Could you just do that again for me please? *(B hesitates. Repeats the procedure)* Mmmmmm . . . Indeed. Interesting. Just once more please. *(Alarmed look on B's face)* Please, just once more.

B. *(Sits again. Again, there's a pause and they inexplicably lose control and fall off)* Can you help doctor? What's happening to me?

A. *(Long Pause)* Well, I'm afraid the news isn't good . . .

30: Awkward Situation

A and B enter mid-conversation

A. I just don't like them.

B. Don't be daft – what's wrong with them? They have been kind to you a few times.

A. Yes, I know all that – it's just. I don't know. Just don't involve me, okay?

B. Don't you think you're being a bit irrational?

A. No, I'm not. Look, count me out will you? Get someone else.

B. And how the hell am I to get a replacement at this stage.

A. I don't know. *(Pause)* I don't like them.

B. Brilliant. You haven't given me one good . . . *(at this point C enters)*

C. Hi, you two.

B. How – how are you?

A. Hi.

C. Fine. What's the news? I'm ready.

    (Brief silence)

B. *(Almost stuck for words)* Nothing much. Everything's all set if you two are.

C. So, let's get to it.

B. *(To A)* You all set?

A. Suppose so. There's nothing you've forgotten?

C. *(To B)* I'm sure we'll make a good team.

B. We'd better do a quick check.

C. Good idea. Won't take a minute.

A. *(To B)* I hope your instructions are crystal clear.

B. Yeah, I think they are.

A.   Look we're in good time. I'm going to get a sandwich. Say we meet back here in about half an hour. *(To B)* Is that okay?

C.   *(With a sense of something not quite right between A and B)* Ahhhh . . . yeah, yeah. That's fine by me.

B.   Yeah, okay.

A.   Grand. See you both in about half an hour so. *(Exits, leaving C and B on stage)*

31: Interrogation

A runs into the acting space, looks back towards offstage. A is apprehensive.

A. *(Loudly, but not shouting, and all the time looking offstage)* Just go away will you? Don't come near me. *(Pause)* Don't take another step or I'll scream. *(Pause)* Just go away. *(Silence. A steps forward trying to see if the threat is gone)* Please. Just go away. *(Silence. A moves and looks around the room a little. There is a chair and perhaps a small table. A is clearly worried. Silence. In direction of other wing)* Anybody there? *(B enters a few steps into space as A's back is turned. B is calm and unthreatening)*

A. *(Turns. Sees B. Quietly)* Please, go away.

B. Take it easy. We should talk. I just want to talk.

A. Stay away. I'll scream. I don't want to talk to you.

B. I don't know why you're panicking. Relax.

A. I thought that was obvious.

B. You're being silly.

A. Please, just go away. I've nothing to say to you.

B. You've been listening to all those stories, haven't you? *(Silence)* Haven't you?

A. What are you going to do?

B. *(Slight laugh)* Do? Nothing. I just think we should talk. *(Takes a few steps)*

A. *(Instantly raises volume)* Don't come near me.

B. *(Conscious of others hearing)* Just a chat, and a few questions.

A. I told you. I can't help you.

B. We can sort this out. I think you can help. And everything will be fine.

A.   *(Looking around briefly)* Others will hear us.

B.   *(Some impatience)* You're making things difficult. Just answer the few questions I have.

A.   *(Pause)* I've nothing to say to you. I'm going. *(Moves towards B to get to exit)* If you lay a finger on me I'll scream the place down. Others will come.

B.   Tomorrow – I'll see you tomorrow. Think about this carefully, okay.

A.   No, no. You just leave me alone. *(Exit. B turns and follows slowly)*

32: Preoccupation – an Improvisation

A is in conversation with B whose responses are improvised. Each response from B must include the mention of a prescribed subject (choose one from list below). *It is important that B makes every effort to fit the subject matter into relevant and plausible responses to A's side of the conversation. In the conversation A's reaction to B's preoccupations can be explored. Initially, play out the scene by having A ignore the incongruities of B's content.*

B is preoccupied by one of the following subjects and feels compelled to get them into their conversation:

- items of underwear;
- melting glaciers in the Alps;
- the English Premiership;
- cycle lanes in Holland;
- bottoms.

The scene opens with A and B sitting at a table in the centre of the acting space.

A.   Let me get this straight. You've given up your computer course and signed up for evening classes about Art History, right?

B.   IMPROVISATION

A.   And I take it you'll work during the day to keep yourself? And what about Thursday night's band practice? You'll be available for that?

B.   IMPROVISATION

A.   Speaking of changes, I'm thinking – only thinking, mind you – of applying for the senior grade that's come up at work. What do you think?

B.   IMPROVISATION

A.   The salary's quite an increase but the workload's the problem.

B. IMPROVISATION

A. Are you planning a holiday this summer?

B. IMPROVISATION

A. I'm not sure myself – have to look at my money situation. You mentioned about a good savings offer you'd seen recently – what was that? I'm going to try and save more.

B. IMPROVISATION

A. I was fascinated by that documentary on Black Holes, absolutely bizarre and kind of spooky.

B. IMPROVISATION

A. So, you've fallen in love with the history of art. Imagine, didn't think you'd be interested in that at all.

B. IMPROVISATION

33: **What do You Want to do?**

A. What do you want to do?

B. I don't know really. What do you want to do?

A. Don't know – whatever.

B. Well, I don't mind really.

A. I'm not pushed.

B. Well, what do you think – I'm easy.

A. What about . . . no, no, couldn't be bothered.

B. Go on, say. I'm game.

A. You make a suggestion.

B. Ahhh . . . let me see. Can't really. Like I say, I'm easy.

A. Me too.

B. Let's go for a coffee and decide.

A. Good idea.
    (Both exit)

34: Yes and No

A.   No.

B.   Yes.

B.   No.

A.   Yes.

B.   No.

A.   Yes, yes, yes.

B.   No, no, no.
      (Pause)

A.   No.
      (Brief pause)

B.   Yes.

A.   I say no.

B.   I say yes.

A.   No!

B.   Yes!
      (Pause. Rapidly)

A.   No.

B.   Yes.

A.   No.

B.   Yes.

A.   No.

B.   Yes.
      (Pause)

A.   *(Almost a whisper)* No.

B.   *(Whisper with hiss)* Yes.

A.   *(Shakes head, slowly, deliberately)*

B.   *(Nods head, slowly, deliberately)*

A.   It's simply not to be.

B.   Yes, it is.

A.   Sorry.

B.   Sorry?

A.   No – it's not to be.

B.   Y.E.S. It is.
     (Long pause)

A.   Negative.
     (Simultaneously)

B.   Yes.

A.   *(Hands over ears. Sings to self)* No, no, no, no, no, no,
     no, no . . .

B.   *(Sings, exciting)* I'm warning you, I'm warning you . . .

35: Gift Shop

During this scene A remains in one place, watching, as the customer browses. B should use the space as if it were a gift shop, perhaps with narrow aisles between shelving, stacked with all kinds of delicate things.

A.   Good day to you. Can I be of assistance?

B.   No thank you, just browsing.

A.   That's perfectly fine. All browsers welcome. That's our motto here.

B.   *(Smiles politely. Begins to browse)* Thank you.

A.   Browsers are the soul of business is what I always say – especially in our line. *(Pause)* Just ask if you need any help. *(Pause. B lifts up something)* Oh, they're particularly nice. Just in yesterday – and very reasonably priced. Wonderful craftsmanship. Or should one say craftsperson. *(Laughs)* Doesn't sound quite right, does it? I love all those bright colours. *(Pause. B finds something else)* Now isn't that a gem? I have one myself. Beautiful. Are you familiar with the potter?

B.   Pardon?

A.   Are you familiar with the potter?

B.   No, no, afraid not.

A.   He lives locally you know.

B.   Really.

A.   *(B lifts up another object)* Now, there's a real treat. Actually, we have them in other colours. There's a selection just in but they're not unpacked yet. It's been very busy recently. I think the red is particularly good though – don't you?

B.   Yes, yes.

      (Pause)

A. Visiting are we?

B. Pardon?

A. Visiting the area?

B. Yes, in a way.

A. How nice *(B picks up another item.)* Very cute aren't they? Very popular indeed. *(Pause)* Just ask if you need anything – won't you?

B. *(Brief pause. B moves around the shop some more)* Actually, there is something you can help me with.

A. *(Perks up)* Yes, fire away.

B. *(Pause, as if what they are about to say has been carefully prepared. Insistent, almost aggressive.)* There's an irritating old fart in this shop who keeps jabbering on and on, giving a running commentary on everything and they won't let the bloody customer browse in bloody peace on this pleasant Monday afternoon. And I just wonder would you be able to get them to shut the fuck up before something awful happens. Do you think you could do that for me? *(Continues to browse)*

A. *(Long silence)* Yes, I think so. I'll see to that. *(A watches B move around the store as if nothing has happened. B goes to exit)* Excuse me, please, just a word.

B. Yes?

A. Goodbye and thank you.

B. Thank you. *(Exits)*

36: Soup

*Two chairs on stage. A sits on one and looks around the
unfamiliar room carefully. They break off scanning the details
of the room for a moment to fix their attention on some kind
of mark on the floor. They then get up and rigorously rub at
the spot with the sole of one shoe. Following this they sit
down and resume looking around again. For whatever reason,
after a few moments, and quite suddenly, A stops this fluid
action and fixes their gaze straight ahead into the audience.
This staring goes on for an uncomfortable amount of time
and is interrupted by what seems to be an insect bite or an
itch. A slaps their neck. Examines their hand for remains. As A
does this, B enters. A hardly reacts.*

B.   Sorry for keeping you. *(Looks at A for a moment)* How
      are you?

A.   *(A avoids eye contact with B for the entire scene)*
      Chowder. Crab, shrimp, sole, hake, whiting – with herbs.
      (Pause) Yummy.

B.   Yes. Lovely. You like soup?

A.   Gazpacho. Onion, bean, shallot, pea, carrot – spicy or
      chilled. *(Pause)* Yummy.

B.   Your favourite?

A.   Mulligatawny. Spices, onion. Hot, hot, hot. *(Pause)* Yum,
      yum, yum.

B.   Have you had a good day?

A.   Borscht Beet root, herbs, garlic – lots of beetroot.
      (Pause) Scrumptious.

B.   Thank you for coming along. I must try some of your
      soups but I wonder would you just tell me a few things
      about . . .

A.   Cock-a-Leekie. Chicken. Creamy leeks. *(Pause)* Yummy,
      yummy, yummy.

B.   Indeed, that sounds very good. We must get you to make some of that. Wouldn't it be nice to have some soup? Maybe after our chat. Now there's an idea, don't you . . .

A.   Madrilene. Sage and tomatoes. Beef and coriander. Very special, very special.

B.   *(Pause. Considers what to do next)* Okay. I think that's enough for today. I might see you again tomorrow. Will you wait here and someone will be along to you. Okay? *(B gets up to leave. Stops. Turns to look back at A, who resumes their staring. B exits. Pause. A looks after B. Returns to staring. Smiles broadly)*

37: A and B and Metaphor

A and B are having a casual conversation after work. A, for some reason, isn't very good with figurative language.

A.   Better watch your job mate. That new fellow is good – he did well.

B.   He did. Like a duck to water.

A.   What?

B.   You know, like a duck to water.

A.   *(Puzzled)* No.

B.   Nothing, just a saying.

A.   *(Vaguely and a little confused. Silence. On safer ground)* Did you watch the match? Bloody disastrous.

B.   Aye, straws in the wind.

A.   What?

B.   Straws in the wind.

A.   *(Again, puzzled. Silence)* They're useless – every one of them.

B.   Headless chickens!

A.   *(Pretends to understand)* Yeah absolutely. And they have two coaches you know.

B.   Too many cooks I say.

A.   Cooks?

B.   Yeah, you know, too many of them.

A.   Cooks? *(Trying his best to follow)*

B.   Yeah, too many of them. I mean the cooks are the trainers – you know, too many trainers.

A.   *(Lost again)*

B.   It doesn't matter. *(Doing his best to give A something to hold on to)* Anyway, you weren't impressed.

B. No. *(Pause)* I can't believe they have two coaches.

A. It might have been a case of falling between two stools. Six nil! That takes the biscuit.

B. *(Thinks seriously before an outburst, after which he storms out)* What the hell are you on about? Biscuits and stools and bloody cooks – and headless chickens! Are you off your bloody head or something?

A. Rocker. Oh, and keep between the ditches.

38: Mirror

*A stands down stage and centre, facing the audience or at
the front of the acting space, in the centre. She is in front of
a mirror. While the conversation with B takes place, A goes
through the actions one might go through in front of a
full-length mirror. Some of these are suggested by the
dialogue but here are a few additions: brushing eyebrows,
examining teeth (front and back), combing fingers through
hair, an attempt at a change of hair style, making faces
(scowl, big smile) brushing clothes, checking dress (front and
back, length, creases, stains), checking size of bottom, hair
cut from the back etc. One of the aims of the sketch is that A
fills the time with natural, seemingly unconscious
front-of-mirror actions while talking with B, who sits to the
left or right of A and a little up-stage. B could be glancing
through a magazine or newspaper.*

A.   *(Standing in front of mirror. B in chair)* Do you know I
      think my eyebrows are getting thicker?

B.   You're just noticing them.

A.   No, honestly they are. And I'm definitely getting more
      nose hair.

B.   That happens to old people.

A.   Well, it's happening to me.

B.   Anyway, is that what you're wearing?

A.   I'm not sure. What do you think?

B.   It's fine.

A.   I don't know. Is it a bit over the top?

B.   No. Why should it be?

A.   I don't know. It just seems that way.

B.   No. You're making too much of a fuss. *(Pause)* How are
      you getting there?

A.   Taxi – just after breakfast.

B.   Have you done something to your hair?

A.   No. Why?

B.   I don't know. Looks kinda different.

A.   I was thinking of getting it cut, really short.

B.   Yeah?

A.   Yeah – maybe, after this – success or no success.

B.   Do you ever think you can see yourself ageing?

A.   All the time. I can see it now standing here. There's a wrinkle I haven't noticed before. And there's my chickenpox mark. *(Points it out in the mirror)*

B.   Oh, is that what that is? Handy if you are ever in a fire or mangled in a crash. We'd be able to identify you.

A.   Lovely. Seriously – what do you think of this? *(Referring to clothes)* Will it do?

B.   It'll do. What's the alternative?

A.   I showed it to you yesterday – the blue.

B.   No. *(Pause)* It really doesn't matter.

A.   It could make a difference.

B.   No it couldn't.

A.   Do you know, sometimes I think my eyes aren't blue at all.

B.   Eye colour won't count either.

A.   I'm nervous you know.

B.   Well stop worrying. You look great.

A.   Seriously?

B.   Come on, get out of that gear and we'll go for a walk and a coffee.

A.   Do you have a receding hairline? Everybody has – no matter what age.

B.   Very funny.

A.   Oh, of course, sorry. Well I think mine's going too, if it's
      any consolation to you. It's getting thin here, on the left.

B.   *(Gets up)* Come away from that bloody mirror will you?
      Let's go. *(Exits. A follows after one last glance)*

39: Monologue and Listener

Throughout the entire episode B says nothing. B's character should be communicated to the audience through gesture, movement within the acting space and expressive voice noise (not words). While performing this any number of pauses can be introduced. A should be prepared to ad lib, using the gist of the speech.

A. . . . you see I told her, I told her and of course she wouldn't listen to me. Needless to say, no sooner had she arrived there when she was on the phone all worried and sick asking me not to switch off my mobile. *(Pause)* I told her she should have gone with her instincts. She didn't even have to go in the first place you know. She told me herself, *(Pause)* he's a weirdo; I don't think I'll go – those were her very words. *(Pause)* Do you know him? *(Pause)* Now she expects me to jump on a plane to rescue her. You should have heard her on the phone. You'd think she was about to be murdered. *(Pause)* I told her to do her own thing and just ignore him. He's just a creep. *(Pause)* Actually, I suggested she phone her boss. No, no, no, she couldn't do that of course. What do you think? She should, you know, if she feels that strongly. *(Pause)* Maybe *I* should phone her boss? *(Pause)* Do you think I'm over-reacting? *(Pause)* Maybe I am. He's a real weirdo. Have you met him? No. They work out of the same office. I've met him. He is bloody odd. You know what I should do. *(Pause)* No, maybe not. *(Pause)* It's typical of her to get herself into a pickle like this. And she could easily have got out of going. Why the hell doesn't she just come home immediately? What difference would it make? Should I phone her? What do you think? And only afterwards it occurred to me that he might think that she was making a pass at him by going. That's possible, isn't it? Isn't it though, when you think of it? That's possible.

40: Returned Visitor

It's a bright sunny day. A, in his early thirties, has walked and scrambled to the top of a substantial hill overlooking the countryside and a small town. Bent over, he breathes in and out heavily for a while before straightening up to take in the view. This takes quite a while. As he does so he takes his knapsack off his back: this can be mimed. He seems to be taking note of certain landmarks. Having looked in all directions, he ends up facing the auditorium, then sits down, stretches out, and uses his elbow to prop himself up. He looks into the distance for a while then sits up, Indian style.

A.   Beautiful. *(With a noticeable sigh, A falls onto his back to look up at the sky. There just might be a sense that A is both relieved and delighted. B, about 17 years old, enters from stage left. She has climbed the same hill. Hands on thighs bent over, she's catching her breath before looking up to notice she isn't alone. A doesn't move; he's fallen into a light sleep. Having studied A for a brief moment, B begins looking around again. Then she decides it might be best to cough a little. There's no response. She realises A is probably asleep. She resumes taking in the view in all directions. She moves carefully around A, checking once or twice to see if she is disturbing him. She ends up at stage right, facing the auditorium. A wakes with a mild fright. B looks around at him and smiles)*

B.   Hi.

A.   Wow, I must have snoozed off.

B.   Sorry, I woke you up.

A.   No, no. It's okay. I came for the view anyway.

B.   Yes, it's incredible.

A.   Yes. *(Pause)*

B.   Are you travelling around?

A.   Travelling around?

B.   Yeah, you know, a tourist.

A.   Yes, I suppose, but I've been here before – about ten years ago.

B.   Up here?

A.   And in the town – I stayed for a few weeks. I'm going to have some coffee from my flask. Would you like some?

B.   *(Slight hesitation)* Yes, that would be nice.

A.   *(Opens knapsack, removes flask etc.)* I always carry two cups.

B.   *(Remains standing. Feels a little awkward)* Have you travelled far?

A.   Today – from Galway.

B.   Is that your bicycle down on the road?

A.   Yeah, but I brought it on the bus. Do you live in the town?

B.   Yes, I live in the house that used to be a shop – the bright blue one. Look, there. *(Points into auditorium)*

A.   *(Brief pause)* I know it. It used to be a pub as well.

B.   That's right. Do you remember it?

A.   Oh yeah, of course I do – 'Bergen's'. Is that your name?

B.   *(While the conversation is going on B is tired standing, but doesn't quite know how to go about sitting down. Eventually she manages it with a little awkwardness. A is oblivious to this)* Yeah. My Dad sold the license.

A.   *(Smiles)* You know, I think we might have met before.

B.   Really? I don't remember much about the shop and pub.

A.   In fact we did meet before-I'm sure of it?

B.   God, isn't that strange? I must have been very small.

A.   You were about nine or ten.

B.   God – that's so funny. You'll have to come down and meet Mum and Dad. Did you know them?

A.　I'd know your Dad a bit. He might remember me. I don't think I met your Mum.

B.　Have you been down there yet?

A.　No, no, I came straight here. I booked into a B & B.

B.　Johnston's?

A.　No, I don't think so. It's called 'The Mill'. It's about a half-mile out.

B.　Oh yeah – they're new. I don't know them. *(Pause)* Did you know Ann and Rodney?

A.　I knew Ann.

B.　Did you? Rodney's in America and Ann's in Belfast.

A.　What's Ann doing?

B.　Something to do with designing books; and Rodney is a kind of guide in the Rockies. He'll be home at Christmas.

A.　Really? Does Ann come home?

B.　Oh yeah. She's always up and down. I've been to Belfast a few times.

A.　Do you know what just occurred to me? Why does a girl like yourself come up here on her own? A boy friend?

B.　I wish. No, just for a walk, and I suppose for a little bit of peace and quiet before tomorrow.

A.　What's tomorrow?

B.　The Leaving Certificate results – final exams.

A.　Oh yeah – I know. The Leaving Certificate.

B.　Yes. That's it. Did you do it?

A.　No. I only lived in Ireland until I was six. Then I went to England. My Dad's English and my mother is German. But I like to think I'm a bit Irish. Anyway – how do you think you'll do?

B.　Okay, I think. I did a bit of work, so I hope I'll do alright.

A.　What'll you do in the future – university?

B.   I'm thinking of taking a year off. Ann has a kind of job for me in Belfast. Then I'll decide for sure.

A.   You'll stay with her?

B.   Yeah. She has a nice flat – well it's an apartment really.

A.   So, you're celebrating tomorrow night then?

B.   Yeah, Mum and Dad are going to take me out early on and then I'll meet up with the gang from school.

A.   Well, I had better make an appearance at my B & B and leave you to your thoughts.

B.   Sure I'll come down with you.

A.   *(Getting up)* Okay.

B.   I'll tell Ann I met you. I'd say she'll phone tonight. Do you have a mobile? *(A is put on the spot)* And you'll have to come in and see Mum and Dad.

A.   Aaah – yeah, I will. I'll be around tomorrow. I'm going to visit an old man a good bit out of town. I used to stay with him. *(Thinking he's escaped)*

B.   Ann will be amazed when I tell her.

A.   Yeah, right, we'll go will we? Are you sure you want to head down?

B.   Yeah, of course.

A.   I feel I've disturbed your contemplation.

B.   No, no, I'm grand.

A.   Okay, we'll head down then. It's almost too good to leave, isn't it? *(Both exit)*

41: Spoofer

A is the interviewer and B is the interviewee. They occupy two chairs, facing each other, centre stage.

A.   Comfortable enough there?

B.   Yes, fine.

A.   You mentioned college – was it in Dublin?

B.   Yes, UCD.

A.   A Bachelor of Arts?

B.   Aaaah, yes – I attended psychology and English lectures – but I didn't take the degree.

A.   Oh, did you drop out?

B.   No, no, nothing like that. I attended almost all of the lectures and read all the course books – far more than necessary actually.

A.   But you didn't finish your BA?

B.   No.

A.   I don't wish to pry, but were you ill?

B.   No, no. *(Pause)*

A.   Sorry, could you just explain why you didn't finish college?

B.   Well I finished my job but not the degree.

A.   Sorry, I don't quite . . .

B.   You see, I stopped going to the lectures when I quit my job.

A.   Your job? In the university?

B.   Yes.

A.   As an employee?

B.   Yes.

A.   You were teaching as well?

B.   No, I was in maintenance – projectors, switches, lights, screens – all that kind of stuff.

A.   *(Surprised but calm and controlled)* So you weren't a student?

B.   No.

A.   Were you ever a student?

B.   No. *(Pause)* But I was at university and I followed a course.

A.   I see. *(Pause. Decides to change direction)* You say you've travelled extensively. Poland, Greece, France, Spain, Russia, Norway.

B.   Yes I have.

A.   Was this valuable work experience or was it all for pleasure?

B.   *(Thinks for a moment)* Yes, I suppose so – both.

A.   Tell me about your time in Poland.

B.   Well, it was really meant to be a holiday in Spain.

A.   So, you haven't lived in Spain?

B.   Yes. I lived there for two weeks.

A.   I see. And Poland?

B.   Well, I stayed in Prague for a night.

A.   One night.

B.   Yes. You see I managed to get on the wrong plane in Dublin.

A.   So, you haven't lived in Poland?

B.   No. *(Pause)* And we got to visit Norway on the way back.

A.   For a night.

B.   No, I think it was about five hours. Even so, it was nice to visit it.

A.   *(Exasperated, but intrigued)* You say you have some experience in journalism.

B.   That's right.

A.   *(Getting into B's way of thinking)* Could you just explain the nature of this experience?

B.   Well I worked on the Evening Standard for a year.

A.   As a reporter?

B.   *(Pause)* No.

A.   An editor maybe?

B.   No.

A.   I see. So, tell me, how did you get this experience in journalism? You weren't by any chance delivering newspapers?

B.   Yes, I was, and I did a little bit of selling.

A.   Right. I think that'll be all for the moment. Do you have any questions?

B.   Aren' t you going to ask me about my experience in broadcasting? It's down there on my CV.

A.   *(Stands)* No, no, that's fine. We'll be in contact, okay? *(B is reluctant to leave. Looks as if he is about to say something)* Thank you very much, I think that'll be all.

B.   *(Stands)* So, you'll contact me? You have the details?

A.   Yes, I have the details.

B.   *(Exits)* Bye – and thank you very much.

42: Talk with Mother

We catch A and B in mid-conversation. There are two chairs in the acting space.

A. Just sit there and be her, for a few moments, and I'll practice how I'm going to do this. *(B goes and slouches in the chair. A about to begin, breaks off. Addresses B as B)* My mother wouldn't sit in a chair that way. Sit up. Sit like her. *(B attempts to sit like A's mother. A watches until satisfied)* Right, are you ready? *(A, as if calling their Mum)* Mum?

B. Yeah? *(Pause)*

A. *(Can't quite believe B hasn't copped on to what is needed)* My mother doesn't say 'yeah'. Say 'yes' – the way she would. Let's start again. *(B has lost their dignified position. Attempts to recover it. A resumes)* Mum?

B. *(Raises the pitch of their voice, but keeping deadly serious)* Yes, darling?

A. Leave the silly voice. *(Pause)* Mum, can I talk to you for a moment?

B. Hold on a minute. You won't have seen your Mum for about three months and you're going to say, 'Can I talk to you for a moment?'

A. No, of course not. I'll pick my moment during the course of the weekend. Now, are you ready? *(Pause)* Mum?

B. Yes darling?

A. *(Looks at B to see if he is taking the task seriously)* Can I talk to you for a moment?

B. Certainly. 'Certainly' – good isn't it? Sounds just like your mother. Can't you hear her? 'Certainly'.

A. Just get on with it, will you?

B. *(Instantly resumes role)* What's the problem, dear? Let me guess, you want to borrow money. *(Mock shock)* I hope you're not in debt.

A. No, no mother. In fact, I'm about to get a very generous raise and maybe promotion.

B. That's brilliant!

A. *(Stopped in their tracks)* Why would my mother use sarcasm?

B. You twit. It's hardly wise to tell your mother about your promotion – or your pay rise.

A. No, I suppose not. Okay. *(Resumes)* No, mother, I'm doing quite nicely really.

B. Well, *(Slightly carried away)* what can Mumsy do for her youngest and dearest?

A. *(Quick glance at B to tell them the last line was a bit over the top)*

B. *(Resumes)* Well, what's the problem dear?

A. It's not a problem really Mum; it's just news really, about Pat and myself.

B. I'm going to be a grandmother – am I?

A. No, no, Mum – although we are thinking about that quite seriously.

B. *(As themselves)* Are you? You never told me. *(A glares at B. A pleads to resume being mother. B resumes)* Go on dear, give me your news.

A. *(Genuinely worried and nervous)* You see Mum, Pat and I were thinking of giving . . . *(B laughs)* What's funny?

B. Your mother's going to hit the shagging roof you know. She won't have thought of this!

A. *(Long pause. Visibly worried)* Yeah, I know.

B. You're really going to tell her this weekend?

A. Have to.

B.   Anyway, go on. *(B settles in chair as mother)*

A.   Mum, Pat and I were thinking of . . . *(Breaks off)* No, that's a lie – we have . . . *(Starts again)* Mum, Pat and I have just handed in our notices and, and – we're going to India . . . *(More to themselves)* with one-way tickets.

B.   *(Not knowing how to react as A's mother. Long pause)* That's an awful lot of news all at once. She hasn't a bad heart has she?

A.   *(Annoyed at the whole predicament)* Look, just react in some way will you.

B.   When? When are you going?

A.   That's enough, Mum.

B.   Don't tell me that's enough. I'm very upset.

A.   *(To B as B)* That's enough. Leave it.

B.   No, I can't leave it. You have to explain yourself. You just can't walk out on us you know.

A.   *(Almost forgetting the role-play)* Mum, I . . . *(To B as B)* Look, just leave it. That's enough. Let's go for a drink.

B.   No, I'm getting the hang of this. Come on, explain yourself. Why are you buggering off to India?

A.   No, no. Come on – let's go.

B.   But you have to have a good explanation – for your mother *(Pause)* Come up with something, can't you.

A.   Would you just shut up? Come on – to the pub.

B.   *(Brief pause)* It's all Pat's idea, isn't it?

A.   Are you coming for a drink or not? And mind your own flippin' business. *(A exits. B doesn't move. A returns, stands close to where B remains sitting)* Are you coming or aren't you? *(A exits again. B follows slowly)*

43: Bearings

A, B and C are all hikers, but A is the most experienced. It is late afternoon and they are nearing the end of a six or seven hour hike of ascents and descents. A, the chief navigator, has miscalculated and misread the ordinance survey map and they have gone astray by a valley and a couple of ridges. This means that the walk turns out to be considerably longer than planned. A enters (stage left) first, purposefully, as a way of disguising the fact that they have gone wrong someway back along the trail. B follows A a few moments later and C a few moments after that. A stops centre stage and takes a brief look at the compass and map. This person is very conscious of time but doesn't want to communicate this to the others. Goes to move on, heading for stage right. B follows, exhausted.

B.   Hold on, hold on. Let's stop here. *(Breathless and very tired)* That was the last ascent – and good riddance. *(Looks up)* What a view! Another hour, at most?

A.   Aaaaa, yeah, maybe. Maybe more. Let's have a look here. *(Looks at map. Thinks aloud to himself. Enter C, absolutely exhausted. C lies down and says nothing during the following exchange)* Ah, you made it. Take a rest there.

B.   *(To C)* Nearly there, my friend. Don't get too comfortable. *(Points into auditorium. Cheered by final run in)* That must be the guesthouse down there – that little cluster of houses.

A.   *(Looks, knowing it can't be. Returns to map)* Let's see here. We went north there and made a descent. Then headed south and came up here . . . *(trails off)*

B.   *(Looks 'down' into auditorium)* I take it that's the path. *(Back to A)* There's a nice sheep path here to get us started – steep enough. God, I'm going to enjoy every drop of my first drink. I can't even think about food. I hope there's a bath instead of a shower.

A. *(Delaying the news that must inevitably come)* Hold on there, I'm not sure that's our valley. *(Looks at compass watched by B. A then points off stage right)* This is us. That gentle slope down. Going west, into the sun – best option at this stage.

B. *(Stands beside A. Looks in direction of A's pointing)* I don't see any houses, or a village.

A. Yep, this is the way.

B. Did I hear you say 'option' by the way?

A. Yeah, it's the quickest route home.

B. Down that meandering path?

A. Yeah.

B. To the wood – and the river.

A. Yeah. That's us.

B. And we cross the river?

A. Yeah, shouldn't be a problem. Might even have a dip.

B. And the village? I'm looking at the other slope and I don't see it. Is it further down the valley? *(Stands close to A. Looks at map)* There's no habitation marked at all. Are you sure we descend here? *(At this point C raises themselves up on an elbow to listen)*

A. *(Points at map)* There. There's the village. *(Looks into distance, off stage right)* Look over there. *(Points)* We cross that ridge.

B. *(Looks at map, then into distance)* Ah, for shit sake, you're joking. Down into that valley and across the next ridge. *(Grabs map)* Look we're here, aren't we?

A. No, we're not . . . We should be, but we're not.

B. Are you sure?

A. Positive.

C.   *(C, who has been propped up listening, returns to flat-on-back position)* Shite-and-onions!

B.   Oh, my God. *(Pause)*

A.   Look, we'd better get going because . . .

B.   *(Snaps)* For bloody hell's sake, would you just wait a minute. I've got to get my head around this.

C.   *(To no one in particular)* No more up hill, please, I just can't.

B.   We went wrong obviously.

C.   *(Again, directed at no one)* My legs are bloody jelly.

A.   Yeah. Remember where we saw the wild goats, way back?

C.   I'm afraid to look at my right foot. It feels like raw meat.

B.   Sorry, let me rephrase that – *you* went wrong.

A.   Followed a path instead of checking the compass – sorry.

B.   The path shaded by the Scots Pine?

A.   Yeah.

B.   *(Situation sinks in. Sits down. Pause)* You're not trying to blame me, are you?

C.   *(To sky)* Please don't tell me how long.

A.   I'm not trying to blame you. I should have checked. That's what I said, okay – we were talking.

C.   Stop wasting energy, will you.

B.   *(Gets up, walks towards stage right and contemplates ridge on other side of valley)* Feckin' hell. I feel sick. *(Returns to where they were sitting)* That's a fairly beefy slope.

C.   *(Groans)* A Mars bar. A Mars bar. A Mars bar might help.

A.   *(To C)* I haven't one. *(Brief pause. To B)* It's do-able – before dark.

B.   And the other option?

A.   Too dangerous.

C. How long, how long – break it to me gently.

B. Bugger, bugger, bugger. *(Pause)* Christ, I'm starving. *(Silence)*

A. Look, we'd better be going. We'll rest down by the wood. *(As if to a larger group)* Come on, come on – let's go. *(Exit stage right)*

B. *(Gets up again and looks at C, who continues to lie flat on their back with eyes closed, then towards stage right. Pause. Angrily)* Get up will you for Christ's sake, or it'll be fucking dark – come on! *(Goes to exit. During this C gets up. C gets ready to move, mentally and physically. We don't hear A's side of the exchange with B as they shout off stage)* How long will it take? *(Can't quite hear)* How long? *(Hears answer – appropriate facial expressions and gestures. Casually to C before exiting)* Half a Mars bar for you down at the river. *(B exits, full of aches and pains. C follows)*

44: Explanations

A.   Look I . . .

B.   It's okay; it's okay; don't say another word.

A.   I . . .

B.   No, no – sit down there.
      (A sits. Silence)

A.   Can I . . .?

B.   Let me explain.

A.   Explain?

B.   Yes. You see, it's like this . . .

45: **Follow the Instructions**

A stands down stage, left or right, and looks out at the audience. B paces back and forth across the stage thinking to themselves. All B's gestures should be exaggerated and as original as possible. This sketch can be as long as you wish. A is in command but should never push B to go on too long with each command, and A should make every effort to vary the duration of each. Tone of voice should also be varied. B should do everything in silence. This idea has numerous possibilities. One is to introduce the 'freeze' command to give B a rest.

A. Stop! *(B freezes)*

A. Think! *(B resumes their striding)*

A. Relax! *(B responds)*

A. Think! *(B again resumes striding)*

A. Party! *(B stops striding; acts appropriately. The above pattern continues below. Each time 'think' is ordered, B strides back and forth)*

A. Think!

A. Sleep!

A. Think!

A. Sail!

A. Think!

A. Conduct!

A. Think!

A. Compute!

A. Think!

A. Repent!

A. Think!

A. Beg!

A.   **Think!**

A.   **Panic!**

A.   **Think!**

A.   **Die!**

A.   **Think!**

46: Potential Love Story in Four Seasons

The idea of this piece is to create the effect of the passing of the seasons, by gesture and action as well as language. A is male and B is female, but it could be the other way around. The opportunity and option to add names into the script is indicated by*. There is a potential to experiment with sound effects in this script.

A.   *(A is on stage, closer to stage left than right. It is outdoors and winter. The temperature is just above freezing. There has been some snow. He is clearing the paths when B enters from stage right. B observes A for a few moments before A becomes aware of B's presence)* Ah, good morning (*), nice to see you out and about. Bracing weather eh? Bracing, but refreshing, I suppose.

B.   Yes. Cold and bright, thank God. Are you keeping well (*)?

A.   Yes, yes, fine as ever. Living on, as they say. More to the point, how are you?

B.   Fine, fine. Getting on with things. Keeping busy.

A.   (*), you've suffered a great loss, you know. You were great pals, your Mum and you. I'm sure you have some lovely memories.

B.   Thank you (*). You're very kind.

A.   Do you know I think it's colder than yesterday. Not a sign of a real thaw.

B.   *(Goes to exit, stage left)* Indeed. And I think my boiler is acting up. We can't be getting cold at our stage in life – can we? *(Stops)* Oh, and thank you for doing my bit of the path – and so neatly (*).

A.   Not at all – nothing like a bit of exercise on a day like this. *(B exits. A shouts after her)* And give me a shout if you need help with the boiler. *(A continues to sweep or shovel snow but gradually his actions change and he is clearly digging and breaking up soil in his front garden. It is Spring. A, by rolling up his sleeves, or taking off a jacket, also might signal the seasonal change. After a few moments, B enters from stage right. She observes A for a few moments before A becomes aware of B and stops to look up from his work)* Do you hear that blackbird (*)? Spring is making its presence felt would you say? I'm sowing some sweet peas today – lots and lots of sweet peas, (*).

B.   (*), you're a tonic. Only yesterday I was thinking how long and cold the winter's been and here's you working away with all the joys of spring. Oh, it's arrived all right (*). And look at the crocuses over there. They're so pretty.

A.   Yes, indeed, the joys of spring. And look at that cheeky little robin. He's building away – oh, off he goes.

B.   And the daffs and early roses are well on the way. I like that orangey rose (*).

A.   They'll be good this year. The crisp, cold weather sets them up. I always imagine they're brighter and bolder for it.

B.   You cheer me up, (*). I'll go about my errands with spring on my mind and a spring in my step. *(Goes to leave. Stops)* You know, there's quite a bit of warmth in that sun.

A.   *(Resuming work)* There is indeed (*).

B.   *(Almost off)* Don't do too much now. Mind that back of yours (*). *(Exits stage left, as before)*

A.   *(Stops what he is doing and turns towards where B has exited. He looks as if he is about to call out, but doesn't. Resumes work – perhaps opening a small seed packet, pouring seed into his hand, making a small drill in the soil etc. Following a few moments of this, A's actions change. Now he does Summer work – clipping hedges, raking grass, mowing the lawn. Now and again he stops work and wipes the sweat from his brow or takes a drink of water. He stops once to smell the air and moves a step or two to bend down and smell a rose. As he's doing this B enters from stage right and watches A for a moment, before he becomes aware of B's presence)* Hot, hot, hot, isn't it (*)? But we mustn't complain, it's lovely to get.

B. *(Suffering a bit from the heat)* Oh, it's hot, but winter will be long enough I suppose. Keeping control of things as usual (*)?

A. Clipping, pruning, mowing – all part of the pleasure.

B. You know I read somewhere that its difficult to keep colour in a garden in July and August, but not for you though. It's a credit to you (*).

A. Ah, you know yourself – I love getting out. It's a kind of company. That's a great straw hat there.

B. *(Pauses to consider this. Goes to exit)* Thank you, thank you. Don't overdo it in this heat now – stop for the odd cuppa. *(Exits)*

A. Oh, I will, I will. *(Almost against his better judgement and almost too late, with voice raised somewhat)* Would you join me in a cuppa now? *(A looks after B. Thinking she's gone, he resumes his task. As he does so B appears)*

B. Did you call after me? (*) *(A, deep in thought)* Did you call after me? Did I hear you call after me, (*)?

A. *(During the following, B's facial expressions are ambivalent)* Yes, yes, I did. Tea. Would you like to share a pot of tea with me (*) in the back garden? In the shade of the magnolia, of course, before you set out and if you're not in a rush. It's just – I'll take your sound advice and it's about the right time and I thought you might join me. Of course, if you're in a rush I wouldn't advise it (*). No point in rushing in this weather. The afternoon's flown and I have the back lawn to do. But there's no point in rushing.

B.   Thank you so much.

A.   You miss the pleasure of things I always say, if you rush.

B.   That's a lovely invitation. But you're right about the rush. Some other time no doubt. *(Exits)*

A.   *(Resuming work)* Certainly, some other time (*). *(A does a summer garden task for a moment and stops. Pause. When he resumes he does a distinctly different action associated with autumn – it could be raking leaves, pruning, digging, picking bulbs. B appears and watches him for a while, until A becomes aware of B watching him)* The leaves, the leaves, (*) they're everywhere. I love it when they're crispy and crunchy. They're a nuisance but I love tidying them up – isn't that funny (*)? Do you like autumn?

B.   Don't mind it I suppose (*). But it's sad at times and has a kind of a lonely feel. *(Pause)* There's a bite in that air alright.

A.   The turning years. Isn't that what they say.

B.   I like your woolly hat (*). *(As she exits)* Indeed, the timely reminders of Autumn.

A.   *(Looks after her. Long pause)* (*), What about that cup of tea? *(Stands on. Doesn't move)*

47: **Second-hand Books**

The scene takes place in a small, academic, second-hand bookshop. A enters carrying a huge holdall of second-hand books they wish to sell. B, the shop owner, is putting books on shelves, checking lists, perhaps looking at a computer screen, moving from desk to shelves around the shop. As the episode goes on B's interest in A goes from interest and curiosity to patient toleration. A is very keen to sell their books and find something to please the shop owner. As A takes each book from the bag they mention its subject, title and maybe the author. The subjects, names and titles mentioned here can be changed to suit the kind of character you imagine selling the books. This handling of books can be mimed or the scene can be done in such a way that A only tells B the books he has to sell, without actually having them.

A. *(Cheerful)* Hello. You buy books don't you?

B. Yes, we do.

A. I'm selling the lot. Would you have a look at them? *(A wastes no time, and rummages in bag to bring out first lot)*

B. Yes, I'll have a look.

A. *(Puts book on desk. B looks through and is not particularly impressed)* These are all to do with sailing. That's very interesting – 'Three Hundred Sailing Stories.' It's very old, I think. *(B picks up another)* That's a book on knots – different kinds of knots. Fascinating. It has photos too.

B. *(Following a further cursory glance)* No, I wouldn't be interested in these I'm afraid.

A. Dictionaries. *(Returns to holdall. Puts dictionaries on desk)* I see you have some old dictionaries over there. I've some here. A Swahili-Japanese beginners dictionary – what about that?

B.   No, I don't think . . .

A.   Or a Russian-Yugoslav tourist pocket dictionary. Hardly
     used. Have a look. Oh, I have a twelve volume
     Do-It-Yourself basket weaving series. It's got nice big
     print too.

B.   I don't think so really. I'd have no call for these.

A.   What about murder stories? I've loads here.

B.   No, we don't do much on thrillers.

A.   Oh. *(Pause)* You wouldn't want any Ladybird books
     either?

B.   No. Sorry.

A.   Right. *(Pause)* I've a couple of nice books on Camogie – a
     great sport you know.

B.   No, I'm afraid not.

A.   *(Slightly forlorn)* Right then. *(B takes on some minor task
     as a means of changing the subject)* And you don't want
     a look at the rest.

B.   No, thank you.

A.   Right. Okay. *(Pause)* Thank you very much anyway. *(A
     packs up bag and exits, watched by B)*

48: Three Voices

Three players, A, B and C, sit or stand in a row facing the audience. A and B can be directed to communicate by facial expression as well as words. There's a different effect created if they don't look at each other. C looks at neither A nor B. There are no stage directions in the script because the tone of voice is the direction. Although the scene suggests that B and C are communicating by mobile, there's no need to have them indicate this by holding them up to their ears. Of course, it is an option. The genders can be swapped around.

A.   I'm not here.

B.   She's not here.

C.   Where is she?

B.   Where are you?

A.   I'm at the pub.

B.   She's at the pub.

C.   Really? That's unusual.

B.   That's unusual.

A.   Colleague leaving.

B.   Colleague leaving.

C.   Strange. She didn't say.

B.   Strange. You didn't say.

A.   Just forgot. Busy time.

B.   Busy time, apparently.

C.   And her mobile must be off.

B.   Your mobile?

A.   Off, broken.

B.   She said something about a new battery.

C.   Oh yeah. How did you hear?

B.   How did I hear.

A.   You were talking to me.

B.   I was talking to her.

C.   Really? Recently?

B.   Recently?

A.   On Sunday.

B.   Yeah, on Sunday I think.

C.   Oh, she never said.

B.   You never said.

A.   I met you on Sunday.

B.   Well, it was Sunday.

C.   Well . . .

B.   Sorry I can't . . .

C.   She's avoiding seeing me you know.

B.   You're avoiding seeing them you know.

A.   Really?

B.   Really? I don't think . . .

C.   Will you be?

B.   Will I be?

A.   What?

B.   What?

C.   Seeing her – will you be?

B.   Seeing you.

A.   Maybe.

B.   Maybe.

C.   I see.

A.   Probably will.

B.   More than likely will.

C.   Soon?

B.   Soon?

A. Later this week.

B. Later this week.

C. I thought you were going away.

B. Mmmm . . . yes, I might be.

A. But you're not, are you?

B. Well, there's a small chance.

C. Tell her I know what's going on.

B. She knows what's going on.

C. You're to say that when you meet.

B. We're to meet.

A. Fair enough.

B. Yes, I'll pass on that message.

C. And will you arrange for us to meet?

B. And arrange for you two to meet?

A. Definitely not.

B. Well, I'm not so sure about that.

C. Why?

B. Well, I mean I'll suggest it.

C. You're in on it too, aren't you?

B. I'm in on it too – aren't I?

A. No you're not.

B. In what? I'm not in anything.

C. That's it then. You can tell her that.

B. That's it then, I can tell you that.

A. Yes.

B. Well, whatever you say.

C. Whatever I say shite. Goodbye.

B. Shite and goodbye.

A. Shite.

49: A Complaint

A.   Ah, good afternoon . . . *(name)*

B.   Yes.

A.   Come in. Now, what seems to be the problem?

B.   I'd like to make a complaint.

A.   Really, I'm sorry to hear that.

B.   Indeed, I'm sure you are. I'd like to complain about your smelly shop assistants.

A.   *(Surprised)* Smell?

B.   Yes, smelly. I don't think they wash.

A.   What kind of smell?

B.   Why, BO of course – a sweaty smell. And feet. There's the smell of feet. Not very nice you know for your customers.

A.   I think you must be mistaken.

B.   I am not mistaken. I use your shop a lot, and well, it's everywhere.

A.   Actually, *(name)* I've just come from the shop, where I've been all morning and . . .

B.   Well then, you must know what I'm talking about. There's the smell of unwashed oxter *(Slight pause)* and foot juice.

A.   I feel you're over-reacting.

B.   Nonsense. I had a good sniff – I know. And you won't have my custom in the future – or anyone else's for that matter – if you don't act soon.

A.   I must say, *(name)*, I'm afraid I think you're over-reacting somewhat and . . .

B.   Come out with me now and smell for yourself. Come on. *(Gets up. Insistent)* Come on and smell for yourself. *(A sits on, not quite sure what to do)*

50: Meeting of Movement

A and B represent two differing kinds of movement on stage. During the dialogue they should make every attempt to move in the way each describes. These 'styles' of movement should be obvious to the audience but not overly exaggerated.

A.   *(Enters first. Moves around stage. Addresses self and audience. Stops. Remains perfectly still, facing audience)* Easy. Smooth. Fluid. Gracefully. Curvaceously. This is how I move. How I move. *(Pause)*

B.   *(B enters, moving around the stage as A speaks. As with A there should be some kind of rhythmical patterning between the movement and the speech. B should end up facing audience about a metre and a half away from A)* Deftly. Sharply. Sequentially. Precisely. Distinctly. This is how I move. How I move. *(Pause. To A)* Oh, hello. You're ahh . . .?

A.   Easiness. Smoothness. Fluidity. I'm 'laconic' at your service.

B.   Yes, I thought so.

A.   And you?

B.   I'm deftness. Sharpness. Sequencing.

A.   Oh, I see. *(During the following conversation A and B should move around a little, subtly demonstrating their respective styles. And when standing still, arm, foot, hand and head movements should in some way indicate movement style)*

B.   Well, how have things been?

A.   Not, bad, not bad. I've been doing a bit of teaching.

B.   Really.

A.   Yeah, one of your types came looking for a lesson. I'm afraid I found it very difficult to get through to them. They shaved the angles, smoothed things out terribly.

Couldn't tell where one movement ended and the next began – all very liquid and loose.

B. Yeah, must be difficult.

A. Well nigh impossible. *(Pause)*

B. Would you like to give it a go?

A. Me?

B. Yeah, and me. I'm sure I can do a bit of fluidity.

A. And I'll try a bit of angling and sharpness.

B. Yeah, let's.

A. I'm not so sure.

B. Ah let's. Nobody's looking.

A. You'll laugh.

B. No I won't. And anyway, you can laugh at me.

A. Will we?

B. Who'll go first?

A. We'll toss. *(Imaginary toss by A, who loses)*

B. Right, off we go.

A. How about simultaneously?

B. Mmmm – okay. Ready. One, two, three. Go. *(Each takes on the other's style, using the full stage. Thirty seconds of this, and they stop. B abruptly; A like a slow fade. Pause)*

A. What do you think?

B. Awful. Doesn't feel right at all.

A. Same here.

(A and B exit, each using the wing furthest away from where they stand)

51: After Beckett

As if thrown from off-stage right, A runs on backwards into space, falls over and tumbles. Gets up, brushes themselves down and looks around.

A.   *(Quite cheerily to audience)* I'll try again.

(Strides off-stage right again. The same thing happens. A is flung back on, they tumble and fall)

A.   *(Thinks. Exits stage left this time. The same thing happens. A gets up, brushes themselves down and looks around. They are slightly worried. Having paused for a moment A heads for stage right again, with real determination. Sudden freeze. Thinks better of the plan. They walk slowly back to the centre of the stage and stop. Looks into the auditorium. Shouts)* Help!

52: Elderly Couple and Ghost

A and B are an elderly man and woman. C is a young man from the woman's past.

A.   *(Sitting on stage. Speaks to B off stage – as if in another room)* Have you put Jasper on the list dear? He's well over his operation.

B.   *(Enters)* Yes, yes, I have Jasper down. He'll be a bit of fun I'm sure.

A.   You know he'd be over fifty years married yesterday.

B.   How do you remember these things? He married young I tell you – younger than us.

A.   Aye. So how many do we have now? Thirty? Forty?

B.   *(B goes to get his list. Counts)* 30 exactly, not including our gang.

A.   Did you confirm the hotel?

B.   Yes, yes dear, it's all done.

A.   Fifty years is a long time.

B.   *(Sits down beside A)* Yes, a long time.
     (Pause)

A.   Do you ever regret?

B.   No – I told you.

A.   Yes I know – but even in the bad times.

B.   I told you dear, even in the bad times.

A.   You're a sweet and a gentle man. We'll have a wonderful night.

B.   We'll get drunk a little and sing songs.

A.   And dance.

B.   And dance.

A.   It'll be worth all the effort, although you were reluctant at first, weren't you?

B. No – just a little lazy. *(Pause)* And you?

A. Me?

B. Any regrets?

A. *(Thinks)* Don't be silly. *(A takes B's hand and holds it. Long pause .C enters)*

C. Yes – you've regrets.

A. It's been good.

C. All the more reason.

A. Did you always love me?

B. Yes, always.

C. You know I always loved you.

A. Strange things, love and loyalty.

B. They don't go away.

C. No they don't. I have never gone away, you know.

A. No, I suppose not.

B. I haven't been a bad husband have I?

A. No, you haven't. *(Pause)* I haven't always been the best.

B. We shouldn't talk about things that upset you.

C. It still upsets – after all this time.

A. Yes, I suppose you're right. I'm sorry. *(Pause)* I'll always feel sorry.

C. All those years, you've loved me.

A. All those years . . .

B. Come on now, don't upset yourself. Let things go.

C. You must tell him.

A. No. I can't . . .

C. You can't live a lie. *(Cuts in)* You must. It's all a long time ago.

A. I will, I will. I have to.

B.   We've been so happy.

A.   Yes, we must let things go. *(A puts her head on B's shoulder. C walks off stage)*

53: Spacecraft

Soh looks into the audience, out through the huge screen of the spacecraft, scanning the galaxy, as if looking for something. Throughout the drama both should have their eyes fixed on the identified object. There should be lots of checking of instruments and flicking of switches. At the end of the scene, or during the entire scene, a third participant might make appropriate sound effects.

Soh: *(Spots something. Urgently into intercom)* Onz, Onz, come quickly, I think I've spotted one; it's coming our way. *(To themselves)* God, this is serious. *(Onz enters running. Stands beside Soh. Looks intently and seriously into the auditorium in the same direction as Soh. Onz is an expert)*

Onz: You're right. It can't be anything else. Shall we tell baseship?

Soh: Look, it's changing colour. Just like they said. Let's not tell anyone.

Onz: *(Soh and Onz give each other a knowing, overly dramatic look)* You're right, let's not.

Soh: This could make us.

Onz: It's shifting course. *(Checks some instruments)* 22 erks away, on a phistotonic line.

Soh: How dangerous Onz? Is it worth the risk?

Onz: Of course it's worth the risk. We can handle it. Adjust our line to 72 erks. Go istotonic. I'm telling you Soh, we can take this one in. We'll be heroes.

Soh: Istotonic? At this speed? Is that wise Onz?

Onz: Sure. Check the prenticks just in case. *(Urgently, Soh goes to some other part of the cabin to check the prenticks. Returns with even greater urgency)* Well?

Soh: Looks okay to me.

Onz: Check the jogs – will you? Since we left I've had a funny feeling about the supply. *(Soh moves across to some other instrument)*

Soh: Four are on half capacity.

Onz: Blast it. I knew. This isn't going to be easy.

Soh: Should we call base?

Onz: Look, Soh it's shifting course. The colour's changing.

Soh: What does it mean Onz?

Onz: It means luck may be on our side. Wait. *(Looks at some very complicated piece of equipment)* Dammit, our fanticure is under pressure – it's faltering.

Soh: *(Looks into auditorium)* It's shifted to 70 reks, Onz. This is dangerous. What are we doing? Change to ginotonic, Onz. This won't work. If we go on like this, we'll be scooded on their razpiece. Come on Onz, ginotonic's the only hope.

Onz: It's too late, Soh. We're scooded. *(Goes to communication system)* Hello base, hello base. This is an emergency. We're being scooded, we're being scooded. Urgent. Help needed.

Soh: The fizzcometre's in the red Onz. What the hell we gonna do? We're beginning break up. *(Onz runs off stage)* Where you going, Onz? Wait for me. *(Exit)*

54: Worried Parent

A and B sit upright, side by side on two chairs. They have their eyes closed. They are in the dark, in bed.

A.   *(Opens eyes. Looks left at imaginary clock at bedside)* Are you awake?

B.   *(Opens eyes)* Yes.

A.   It's quarter to three.

B.   Is it?

A.   She said she'd be back at around half one.

B.   She's fine. She'll be back soon.

A.   She's over an hour late.

B.   She'll be back. *(Pause. A and B stare straight ahead in the dark)*

A.   Will you drive in to see?

B.   She'll be back soon I'm telling you.

A.   She should be home. Go on, you'd better.

B.   Look she's fine. She said she'd take a taxi.

A.   Please.

B.   Look, just leave it – go to sleep. *(A and B freeze. C and D enter. They move downstage. They've been running and are breathless)*

C.   You' better go soon. I don't want your parents annoyed with me.

D.   It's fine. I said around two.

C.   Are you sure?

D.   Very responsible aren't you?

C.   Yeah, well?

D.   Responsible and cute.

C. *(Laughs)* Of course I am. Cute?

D. *(Slightly coy)* And gorgeous.

C. That's me.

D. *(Obviously very happy)* We've known each other for all of five hours.

C. Yeah – but it was quality time. Hadn't you better go?

D. Come on then Mr Responsible – walk me up. *(C and D Exit. When C and D exit one wing A and B get up and exit opposite. D re-enters. She is in her house on her way to bed. B. enters from opposite wing)*

B. God, where the hell were you? You mother's worried sick. You should have called. Did you have your phone?

D. It wasn't charged.

B. Where were you?

D. At the concert.

B. I mean 'til now.

D. Look Dad, would you give over – what's the fuss about?

B. I just wish you'd stick to what you say.

D. If you really want to know I met this wonderful guy – he gave me a lift home.

B. You took a lift home from a complete stranger?

D. Dad!

B. You'd better not tell your mother.

D. I'm nineteen!

B. I don't care. We're only human – we worry.

D. I'm sorry. *(Pause)* I'm here now okay? And I haven't been assaulted.

B. You'd better go up to your mother. *(Pause)* And don't mention about the lift home.

D. For goodness sake, Dad, I'm not pretending.

B. Whatever you think. But she can't stop thinking about that weirdo last month.

D. *(Leaving)* I'm going up to Mum – okay?

B. *(Sighs)* Goodnight.

D. Goodnight Dad. *(Exits, followed by B)*

55: **Angry not Angry**

A. *(Enters. Something has caused an upset. They shout for B)* Hey!

B. *(Enters. Mild surprise at tone)* What?

A. Sit down.

B. *(Sits. Turns very serious)* What?

A. What's wrong?

B. What's wrong with you?

A. Nothing. I just want a quick word.

B. You're angry.

A. No, I'm not. I just want a quick word.

B. Okay – what's the quick word?

A. Take it easy. *(Pause)* You moved the furniture.

B. Yes.

A. Last night?

B. Yes.

A. But you never said.

B. That's right. *(Anticipating A's reaction)*

A. Yes, but . . .

B. As agreed, as agreed. My turn, remember?

A. Yes, but . . .

B. *(Very irritated)* God, I can't believe this.

A. *(Goes to say something but doesn't. Exits)*

56: Charity

A is on a busy footpath collecting for a charity but they are not having much success. Before B and C appear the scene opens with imaginary shoppers walking by on the footpath. A holds out the collection tin and turns in different directions to catch the eyes of those walking past. The collector is despondent and after a moment gives up trying. A considers. Decides to try something different when B enters from stage right and makes their way across the stage.

Using a collecting box for this scene would be more effective.

A.   *(Follows very closely behind. Shouts)* Oi you! *(B, unaware of A, freezes with fright, then turns around. A, quietly, to B)* Would you like to help Meals on Wheels?

B.   You frightened the bloody life out of me. What the hell are you at?

A.   Sorry, but would you like to make a contribution?

B.   No, I wouldn't. Go away. *(B turns away. Exits)*

A.   *(A considers. Decides this tactic isn't appropriate. C enters from stage left. Walks past A who responds immediately with a new tactic. Turns and walks in the same direction as C. Halfway across the stage A suddenly goes down on their ankle and falls to ground)*

C.   *(Surprised. Concerned. Helps A up)* Are you okay? That was a nasty fall.

A.   Oh boy, that was a shock. I'm fine. I'm fine. *(Quickly followed by)* Would you like to make a donation?

C.   *(Looks at A and then at collecting tin)* Sorry?

A.   Would you like to make a donation?

C.   *(About to put hand in pocket. Thinks twice)* Did you just . . .?

A.   Pardon?

C.   You did, didn't you?

A.   It's for Meals on Wheels?

C.   *(Turns. Exits)* God, you're pathetic.

A.   *(Shouts after)* Please. *(Moves up stage centre. Sits on floor)*

57: I'll Phone You on Monday

A is in a shop to inquire about a plastering trowel they had to return the previous week because the handle broke. The boss, who took back the trowel, isn't available but has left a message to say that they phoned the manufacturer in search of a replacement. A is annoyed about having to wait further, and at not being able to see the boss. B and C are shop assistants. B is fairly patient, but C is more off-hand and direct, and is off-stage at the beginning of the scene.

B.   Sorry but the boss isn't here.

A.   Will they be in at all today?

B.   No, not until Monday.

A.   It's about the trowel I left here last week – the one with the broken handle. I was just wondering if there was any news?

B.   Well, I know they phoned the manufacturer about it.

A.   That was a very expensive trowel.

B.   Well, I'm sure it'll get sorted out.

A.   Will they give me a replacement?

B.   You'll have to wait until the boss gets back really – on Monday.

A.   But I can't be travelling in all the way. They should give me a replacement.

B.   I can't really say. You'll have to wait. Monday. We'll let you know on Monday.

A.   That's no good to me now.

B.   *(Reassuring)* I'll phone you on Monday to let you know, or the boss will.

C.   *(Enters having over-heard some of the conversation)* Boss won't be in until Monday.

A.   What good is that to me?

B.   If you give me your number, I'll phone you on Monday.

A.   I came in today thinking I'd get a replacement.

B.   Well I'm sorry but . . .

A.   Can you phone the company?

B.   They'd be closed today – Saturday. *(Fixes A with a gaze)*

C.   That trowel had a fall. That's what the fellow said on the phone – the handle's broken.

A.   That was brand new you know.

C.   A fall is a fall.

B.   I'll phone you on Monday to let you know.

A.   Can you give me some sort of a replacement now?

C.   A fall is a fall – new or old.

B.   *(Cuts across C)* We'll phone you on Monday, okay?

A.   That trowel was forty pounds – a week has passed and it's still not settled.

B.   I'll phone you. I'm sure everything will be okay.

A.   How will I know about the replacement?

C.   A fall is a fall I'm telling you. I don't think you'll get one.

B.   *(Attempts to wind things down)* If you give me your number I'll phone you – on Monday, first thing.

C.   *(Half to themselves)* The most expensive golf club in the world might break with a fall.

A.   I only had it for a day or two. They're meant to be very durable.

B.   Look, I'll let you know on Monday. Write your number down there.

A.   And will the boss not be in at all today, because . . .

C.   There's nothing he can do anyway.

A.   *(Writes number)* It says 'durable' on the package.

B.   That's great. I'm sure it'll turn out fine.

C.   *(Exiting)* Well, I wouldn't be so sure. That must have been some fall. *(Laughs)* Were you up on a skyscraper?

A.   *(To B)* I bought the most expensive one deliberately. You'll phone me on Monday won't you, first thing?

B.   Yes, as soon as I can get an answer.

A.   That trowel was only . . .

B.   Monday then – right? *(A stands for a moment. Leaves slowly)* You'll hear from us on Monday. Bye now.

58: Mystery

A. *(Enters slowly, stage right. Tentative voice. Moves towards centre stage)* Hello? *(No response)* Hello?

B. *(Enters stage right)* Yes?

A. I'm looking for Mr and Mrs King. I received a note . . .

B. Ah yes, good. Let me get some chairs. *(Exits)*

A. Thank you. *(Looks around)*

B. *(Enters with two chairs)* Here we are.

A. I'm . . . . *(Gives name)* I got a . . . *(Hesitates)* . . . I received a note from Mr and Mrs King.

B. Ah yes. *(B looks slightly overlong at A)* Good. Thank you for coming.

A. Yes. *(Unsure of what's to happen next)*

B. We . . . eh . . . I . . . eh . . . I. *(B stops. Pause)* You look remarkably like your mother you know that?

A. Did you know her?

B. Yes, yes, I did indeed – anyway, you're here.

59: Young Child and Parent – Version 1

A is a parent. B is a young person between the ages of 10 and 12 years old. The family pet of ten years, a dog named Sam, has died quite suddenly. A has to tell B. The furniture is a table and two chairs. B enters, having been at school all day and is tired but perky. Enthusiastic about an astronaut who has visited the school. B moves around the space as a young child would. A tries to control their feelings but we can read the upset when they enter.

B. *(Enters)* Hello all! *(Listens)* Anyone here? Mum? Sammy boy?

A. *(Enters from opposite wing)* Hi there! That was quick. Are you early?

B. Yeah, a bit. We got out early 'cause of the astronaut talk.

A. Oh yeah?

B. Yeah, it was brill. There was big speakers and sound effects and a big screen. And she was very funny.

A. A woman?

B. Yeah, she was cool.

A. So, you'll want to be an astronaut now.

B. *(Finally sits at table with drink)* No, but I'd like to go into space sometime. Is Sam outside?

A. Darling, I've some sad news to tell you.

B. Yes? Is Gran ill again?

A. No, no, Gran isn't ill. Gran's fine. No, it's Sam. After you left this morning, Sam got ill.

B. He was okay when I got up.

A. Yes I know, but he got ill. He was acting very strangely, so I called the vet. And I'm afraid he died just before lunch – at the vets. *(Pause. Silence. B looks intently at parent to see how they are reacting. A watches B also)* It's so sad darling. The vet said he was lucky to go when he did – it was a kind of heart attack.

B.   *(Tries to take in fact)* Were you there?

A.   No, I wasn't. *(Silence. Pause. B's feelings well up. He gets up and exits quickly)* Darling, wait. *(Shouts after B)* The vet said he wouldn't have felt any pain . . . *(A sits on)*

60: Young Child and Parent – Version 2

A is a parent. B is a young person between the ages of 10 and 12 years old. The family pet of ten years, a dog named Sam, has died quite suddenly. A has to tell B. The furniture is a table and two chairs. B enters, having been at school all day and is tired but perky. Enthusiastic talk about an astronaut who has visited the school. B moves around the space as a young child would. A tries to control their feelings but we can read the upset when they enter.

B. *(Enters)* Hello all! *(Listens)* Anyone here? Mum? Sammy boy?

A. *(Enters from opposite wing)* Hi there! That was quick. Are you early?

B. Yeah, a bit. We got out early 'cause of the astronaut talk.

A. Oh yeah?

B. Yeah, it was brill. There was big speakers and sound effects and a big screen. And she was very funny.

A. A woman?

B. Yeah, she was cool.

A. So, you'll want to be an astronaut now.

B. Were you crying?

A. Yes, darling. I was crying.

B. Why were you crying?

A. Something very sad has happened. *(Child's name here maybe)*

B. Don't be sad.

A. It's because of Sam. I had to call for the vet after you left this morning.

B. Did he die?

A. He was acting very strangely and the vet took him to the surgery.

B.   Did he die?

A.   Yes, darling he did – about lunchtime I got the call.

B.   Why didn't you get me from school?

A.   Because I thought he might be okay and you had that talk I suppose.

B.   Can I see him? I want to see him.

A.   *(Hesitant)* Yeah, maybe, I'm not sure. We'll have to call. *(A looks at B carefully)*

B.   You should have collected me. I want to see him. *(Gets up. Exits quickly. A sits on)*

Late Night Coffee Shop: An Improvisation Exercise

This exercise and the process that goes with it can take a long time to master but much depends on a groups understanding of the cooperative nature of dramatic improvisation. So, some short preparatory exercises on improvisation may be necessary. Everyone need not participate (group dynamics and experience matter here) and those who don't can be the audience; however, if all goes well, those who are reluctant, having watched for a while, may finally volunteer to take on the role of one of the collection of characters who pay the coffee shop a visit.

The stage space becomes a late night coffee shop in the middle of a city, near a station, cinemas, theatres, apartments. The necessary furniture is two or three small tables or flat desks and about six chairs. As props, it is helpful (but not essential) to have cups and a few side plates, and maybe a newspaper.

The coffee shop will have a worker and various characters (the clientele) who will be there from the beginning or will enter and leave during the course of the improvisation. Each character, along with their imagined profile or background will be allotted to the students who wish to participate. Those who are not in the improvisation become the audience along with those who participate but join them after the scene has begun, playing their respective roles.

Step 1

Before explaining the setting to the students ask for a volunteer to leave the room. Although the person who leaves the room will know they're to be involved, they shouldn't yet know that they're to be the coffee shop worker – a character central to the whole exercise and whose role and brief is outlined in Step 3 (see below). Of course, if the exercise is repeated the subsequent café worker will be aware that this is their job but they won't be aware of the kind of characters they're going to come up against. The student who plays the coffee shop worker's part should, ideally, be fairly willing to enter a role. The other members of the group who volunteer will be given a character to play in the improvisation.

Step 2

When the coffee shop worker has left the room the other participants are allotted their various parts with a full explanation as to how and why each of them has ended up in the coffee shop at this hour. Of course, it is important to invent other characters to have an interesting and varied clientele in the coffee shop at any one time. Here are some of my favourites:

Brother and sister meet late at night to discuss their difficult mother. Both are very busy people. It's the sister's turn to have mother for a week but she wants to change the arrangement – something she's done a number of times before – as her partner and herself, at short notice, have the opportunity to go on a holiday at a knock down price. Her brother has had mother for a week in the fairly recent past and is very reluctant. Those who take on each character must cooperate in order to sustain their negotiation in the coffee shop. Before they begin they should agree the outcome so that their dialogue can work in this direction after a number of detours. They might also agree among themselves at what point they're going to leave (See Step 3).

During their discussion each, at different times, should ask the coffee shop worker for more coffee, a piece of cake or a sandwich. If they are refused, one or both of them might persist with their request. Maybe their mother is the mother who is the subject of discussion in the script, *Talk With Mother?*

Old woman sits alone at one of the tables in the coffee shop. She is very quiet. She lives near the coffee shop in an apartment on the third floor. She is the woman from the script *Dead Dog*. At some point she gets very upset and cries to herself but can be heard by others. She too asks for more coffee and maybe more cake to comfort herself (be specific about the kind of cake). If she is the last to leave the premises she might tell her story and ask the student worker to come to her apartment to help her get the dead dog down the stairs. She might also ask the student to dig a grave for the dog in a garden at the rear of the building. The student worker has to cope with this and try to close up.

Busybody wants another cup of coffee and complains now and then about small petty things – a detail in the toilets, the consistency of the cake, the heat – not all at the same time. This is the kind of character who might interfere in the conversation of others. Suggest that the old lady does this if the discussion between the sister and brother gets too loud. She might tell them to be quiet or she might ask about the argument and take sides or offer advice.

The fairly well mannered drunk (but not utterly legless) man or woman enters in the middle of the proceedings following a prompt from the facilitator. They should enter through the agreed doorway. As they are coming from the audience this imagined entrance should be by way of the 'auditorium' centre aisle into the stage space. This character has been in the coffee shop earlier in the afternoon and is in search of a lost wallet. They have a look around and engage the coffee shop worker by asking a number of questions about whether or not the wallet has been found or handed in. Of course, the drunk eventually asks about the possibility of having a cup of coffee and something to eat, doing their best to persuade the coffee shop worker to cooperate, even though it is closing time. The drunk may or may not get their way. The drunk's time to give up trying might be signalled by the facilitator or if the coffee shop worker threatens to call the police. Remind the student playing the drunk that their presence and movement in the space is as effective as what they say and they shouldn't feel the need to talk continuously.

A foreign tourist backpacker (maybe two of them) type also enters the coffee shop, mid action, through the agreed doorway, before or after the drunk. The tourist has very little English and needs some help with directions to their hostel. They, like the drunk, should look for the coffee shop worker's attention. They too might ask for a cup of coffee and something to eat.

The lover boy or girl can be in the coffee shop from the beginning or enter soon after the scene begins. Their brief is to become, very subtly, more and more friendly to, and more familiar with, the coffee shop worker. It's a good idea to have them end up as the last customer to leave, when they might take the opportunity to ask the worker for their phone number or ask them for a date. This character too will ask for another cup of coffee.

The very strange person's brief is to be more of a presence in the café and to say very little but to, at some stage, ask for another cup of coffee. Perhaps this character might sing to themselves or make quiet grunting noises. At some stage they will simply leave. When doing so they might attempt to shake hands with the coffee shop worker and some of the clientele. Again, stage presence is the more important part of the dramatic effect.

The police officer may have to be called upon if the coffee shop worker feels that they are being threatened or that one of the customers is in danger; or, if it's the case that someone cannot compromise or negotiate and simply refuses to leave. Try to avoid the latter. If this does happen the character causing the trouble is arrested and taken away.

Step 3
Once the roles have been allotted and a number of characters have taken their respective places in the late night coffee shop, the improvisation can begin. I always begin with the busybody, the old lady with the dead dog and the arguing siblings. The coffee shop worker is then brought back into the room and their brief is explained to them. It might go as follows:

> *It is a late night coffee shop and you're a long time, experienced student worker in the place. It is about ten minutes to closing when the action begins. You have customers but you're preparing to close up – sweeping the floor, collecting unused cups, wiping tables etc. Your brief is to have the customers leave and close up shop as near to time as possible. When the action starts you – the coffee shop worker – are at the kitchen with your back to the audience. From the command to start, count down a slow five in your head before turning around. This allows every one to get into their respective roles. From the start your job, at this time of night, is to clear up, empty the shop and go home.*

Some advice for a facilitator:

- Strongly emphasise to all participants that improvisation is an exercise in cooperation. Cooperation to create various kinds of tension between characters for the benefit of the audience.
- Remind participants that they are strangers to each other. Therefore, there should be no inappropriate physical contact. For example, the coffee shop worker can't drag clients out of their chair in order to close the place.

- Watch the action for moments where an exchange between characters has run its course and needs to take a new direction. This might be the time to signal for the entry of another character, by a change of tone or a different kind of language or gesture.
- Warn the actors that you might call 'freeze' at any time. When this is done those in the acting space should freeze in their positions, to allow time for the facilitator to redirect the action, point out a successful or interesting gesture or line or to break up a silly verbal stalemate. With the right timing this kind of intervention can help sustain the momentum of the scene. If the facilitator comes on stage to direct, they are invisible. Tell students to keep the improvisation going if you shout instructions from the side but don't actually freeze actions and move into the acting space.
- Intervene if there's a stalemate between characters and point a way out of it. Point out that improvisation is not about the actors winning a sparing competition but about creating entertainment.
- Loosely agree beforehand how long a character might stay on stage before leaving the coffee shop, and how they might leave.
- Suggest which character will be last out. Ending with two on stage allows for a quiet scene after all the talk and movement. Of course this will depend on which character is last out.
- If a character is tiring in their role simply suggest that they find a way to leave the coffee shop in character.
- Beware if the character has no intention of getting into a role and is only there to get at one of their mates.
- The coffee shop door can be locked (by mime) if the worker has the wit to do this. This of course might prevent the drunk's entry for example, in which case the drunk can knock on the door (mime by stomping foot) in an effort to get someone's attention.

Finally, the energy, tension and humour that can be generated in this improvisation relies on the pressing need of the coffee shop worker to have the place closed for the night, but on the way this need is thwarted by the customers and their need to have a cup of coffee and say what they want to say. Call a halt to the exercise when it is going well, before the energy and sense of theatre flags. Allow time for feedback – a discussion on the difficulty of improvisation, the kind of cooperation it demands, some response from the actors as to how they feel their various characters were treated.

As mentioned above, invent more characters. Give them a story. Play with the combination of characters in the coffee shop. As facilitator, hone your skills at intervening in the improvisations with the aim of improving the dramatic piece. Sometimes, freeze the action and ask the audience for directorial suggestions that might improve the overall impact.